Gobi Runner has entered the boardroom

"Stéfan's desert adventures have taught us all about overcoming adversity and how to beat the bad news and win. This book is a manual on focus. A must read."

–Jim Warrington, Executive Director, NABS Canada

"… inspiring from start to finish."

–Chris Wood, Chairman, GBO Inc.

"Your life is what you choose it to be. Reflecting this philosophy, Stéfan provides an excellent reminder that anything is possible when you choose to put your soul into it and refuse to fail."

–Howard Breen, President HBideation,
author of A page from a CEO's Diary

"This incredible story was highly motivational and had a significant impact on my life. Seeing what Stéfan was able to accomplish once he put his mind to it made my personal goals seem much easier to achieve. If you are looking for a way to inspire your team, this presentation will do it!"

–David Civiero, CEO, The Link-Line Group of Companies

"A unique and entertaining perspective on issues and realities we are facing in our business lives, presented in a practical and engaging format. Our teams will apply several learnings from Stéfan's presentation in both their personal and professional challenges."

–Andy Querin, President, KB Media

"I have heard Stéfan's story a number of times and never cease to be amazed. His story inspires me as a leader, inspires me as a manager, and inspires me as a human being. I learned from his presentation and it has encouraged me to step up my game physically and mentally. I have now signed up for a race of my own."

–Patrick Sullivan, VP & General Manager, ComFree

"We had the privilege of having Stéfan speak to our team during a company-wide meeting. It had been a fast-paced, challenging two quarters at FUSE where our team was feeling the obstacles of agency life (growth, change, client demands, etc.). *Gobi Runner* is about finding courage to face life's obstacles and Stéfan's approach to pushing your own personal boundaries was very gripping. He delivered his speech in far more of a story-telling approach than a speech – an approach that was welcoming, humble, and engaging for the entire team. The story of his journey was filled with a mix of big, life-changing discoveries contrasted against minute and humorous observances from the road ... all connecting back to real-life business learning. When he finished he had our team wanting more. I'd welcome him back any day."

–Stephen Brown, President, FUSE Marketing Group

"As a long-time friend of Stéfan, I remember clearly when he threw down the gauntlet and said he was going to do this incredible run for a great cause. He accomplished a nearly impossible feat, dealing with everything from excitement, trepidation, and mental and physical pain to get to his goal. Simply inspiring."

–Sean Shannon, Managing Director,
Expedia Canada/Latin America/Australia/New Zealand

"Within us all survives that child with the 'crazy' dreams and 'unreasonable' ambitions. May we all, like Stéfan in this book, allow that child to flourish."

—Mehmet Danis, winner, Atacama Desert Crossing

"*Gobi Runner* is highly motivating and makes one realize that virtually anything is possible with focus, determination, and a passionate commitment to achieving a goal. There are numerous lessons here for anyone who is fortunate enough to hear Stéfan's story."

—Kevin Young, President, Armtec

"*Gobi Runner* brought some perspective to what adversity really means in a year when all of us have had our share of difficult situations to deal with. What Stéfan delivered was more than I could have ever have expected. The life lessons that he communicates in his presentation are applicable to all ages, levels, and walks of life. Our team walked away inspired, motivated to do more personally and professionally, and in awe of what one person can do if they set their mind to it. I would highly recommend that you invest the time in your people."

—Brent Lowe-Bernie, President, comScore

"Stéfan has pushed the boundaries and found his new 'normal' while continuing to lead his business and family. In so doing he has inspired me to reach a little higher and consider the ways I can achieve my personal adventures."

—Shaun Francis, CEO, Medcan Health Management

"All leaders can draw from Stéfan's presentation. From the depths of one's being is where leadership, courage, and determination are born. *Gobi Runner* is awe inspiring!"

—Craig Campbell, CEO, Total Security Management

"Sharing the story with us was nothing short of 'ultimate inspiration.' Thank you! You made us proud to be associated with you. *Gobi Runner* invokes a certain spirit in all of us."

"*Gobi Runner* reveals numerous insights for me about a close friend and business partner of the past 25 years. What the book does not reveal is the positive transformation that Stéfan's quest had on Mandrake the company. Stéfan's ultramarathon in the desert created a sense that no task in the office was impossible."

"Stéfan teaches us that perseverance, combined with proactively managing one's own mind and expectations, while holding fast to an inner belief in one's inherent ability to reach one's full potential, breeds incredible (and often surprising) positive results. In a word, Stéfan is inspirational. He exemplifies a profoundly successful approach to life."

"Although I resisted the invitation to join Stéfan on his first desert run (and each one since!), as a work colleague and a friend I have seen the commitment that Stéfan has brought to these projects. It takes courage to do what he is doing and I have heard the stories of the 2 a.m. training runs and the injuries from him firsthand. Few of us would have foreseen, three years ago, how Stéfan would use his experience to inspire the community by turning it into a fundraiser, a presentation, and now a book."

"*Gobi Runner* takes you on a roller coaster ride that is hugely inspirational while retaining a vulnerable personal touch that we should all be able to relate to as we reach for our own personal and corporate goals. Stéfan shares his quest with others so they, too, can be inspired."

—*Bruce Levitt, CEO, Levitt-Safety Limited*

"I followed Stéfan's blog during his journey across the Gobi and was truly inspired on a daily basis by reading what he was going through. His presentation on his emotional and physical journey will captivate your imagination and touch your spirit. Perhaps it will even ignite an inner flame to accomplish the impossible. *Gobi Runner* illustrates what humans are capable of achieving; it is a great vehicle for motivating individuals and teams."

—*Sandra Hokansson, President and Country Manager, Adecco*

"Stéfan's presentation describes his intense personal experience in conquering his challenges and fears in the Gobi Desert, but for the audience it is much more than an adventure travelogue. Rather, through Stéfan's powerful story journey of self-discovery, we see a real-life metaphor for our own search for meaning and purpose in our personal and professional lives as we seek to find our own Gobi experience."

—*Tom Reeves, CEO, Interface Biologics*

"'... great presentation ... made me want to push myself much harder, in every aspect of my life, to achieve the goals I have set.' With only exceptional feedback like that, I hope you'll make many more of those presentations. Thanks again for sharing."

—*Claude Carrier, Co-Owner, Bos*

"… inspiring and truly remarkable. A great source of motivation."

–Jean Noelting, CEO, RoyCap

"People were inspired by not only what you did but what it took to do it. Several came up to me later with thoughts and ideas of things that they have put off in the past and now are going out and 'doing it.' I try my best to inspire the staff and keep the morale positive. Certainly last year was not an easy task, but this presentation was great and it certainly worked."

–Anita Dong, President, McDonnell Haynes

"*Gobi Runner* is a fascinating experience – on both a personal and physical level. The scope of the race's physical and emotional demands on the participant is enormous. What has been more interesting has been the learning that Stéfan shares. He has created an interactive presentation that highlights the individual and corporate challenges that many of us face in the business world. He has developed a powerful hands-on list of easy-to-understand life-lessons that are applicable to both an entrepreneur and a Fortune 500 CEO. Having experienced it, both at the board level and for staff team-building exercises, I've seen how each time the participants have expressed that the content and his personal message have impacted them and motivated them to look for new ways to rethink their personal goals in life."

–Mike Fenton, Director Principal Gifts, West Park Healthcare Centre Foundation, Past President & CEO, NABS Canada

GOBI
RUNNER

Taking a
Personal and Professional
CHALLENGE
to the Desert

STÉFAN DANIS

BPS books

Toronto and New York
www.bpsbooks.com

Published by
BPS Books
Toronto, Canada
www.bpsbooks.com
A division of Bastian Publishing Services Ltd.
www.bastianpubserv.com

ISBN 978-1-926645-79-7

Cover: Gnibel
Front cover photograph: Zandy Mangold /
www.racingtheplanet.com
Author photograph: Darlene Huynh

Text design and typesetting:
Daniel Crack / Kinetics Design
www.kdbooks.com

To my mother and father:
Thanks for the sacrifices you made for me,
bestowing me with good legs, helping me
develop abundant resilience, always telling me that
anything is possible, and providing a caring and
loving environment for me to grow up in.

CONTENTS

PREFACE

Gobi Runner is my account of why I, the CEO of a company caught in a devastating economic recession, signed up for a 250-kilometer foot race in the desert without having run a marathon before. In it I detail the emotional and physical breakthroughs and breakdowns I experienced in preparing for, training for, and running the race. It also explores my reentry into a life that was changed forever.

Besides being a personal story, this book includes the incredible tales of the other participants in the race and the lessons learned by many of us. It details what really goes on to get you through a race in such extreme, adverse conditions; these include visualizing success, owning up to fear of failure and success, taming your inner critic, befriending adversity, collaborating while competing, and learning to enjoy the journey more than reaching the destination.

I may have done the actual running, but others supported me. To my wife, Leslie, thank you for taking on more than your fair share to keep the family going and for providing so much emotional support. You, along with Montana and Jade, were with me every step of the way.

This book would not have been written if Sean Shannon and Jim McKenzie hadn't urged me to do so, and if Steve Phillips hadn't encouraged me to present the story at a Young President Organization event. Thank you, gentlemen.

My thanks to: Dijana Ebach for providing constant ground support, from beginning to end; Jim Warrington for broadcasting the message; my Mandrake and NEXCareer partners for their support, especially Daphne Bykerk; Mehmet Danis and Donna Carrigan for all the mentoring; my YPO forum for sparring with me over the project and kicking in some cash; Dr. Kazemi, for putting me back in one piece when my conditioning looked so bleak; Phil Delaire for training; and, finally, Ernie Votis and Luigi (Louie) Santaguida for making the trip across the world to run the Gobi, and the race itself, such a memorable experience.

National Advertising Benevolent Society team members do an amazing job of helping the community and did so through this project as well. Thank you, Mike Fenton, for supporting my vision, and Louise Bérubé and Jim Warrington, for their boundless energy and for reading and commenting on the manuscript.

Thanks to all of you who pledged and who encouraged me along the way.

PROLOGUE

With a bit of time on my hands, I was antsy, unable to be in the moment. I was tired and unsettled. I was unhappy. I wandered to a stream nearby – it was the one of the first times that there was any water close to camp. Desperate to bathe, I started cleaning my gear and de-taping my mummified upper body: shoulders, hairy chest, back, and abdomen, then my shins, heels, the bottoms of my feet, and my toes. Like an oversized duck splashing in a tiny puddle, I waded into seven centimeters of water. I had the whole stream to myself. Heaven, I thought. It was my first true moment of privacy during the race.

I filled my lungs with air, counted to eight, then pushed the air out, counting to sixteen, trying to put myself in a meditative state, trying to slow time down so I could capture a beautiful moment in the middle of the desert. The only expectation I had before starting the race was at least to complete it, and now I could almost smell the finish line.

Thirty minutes later, *implosion*. The universe conspired to give me what I had essentially asked for. I had checked out of the race physically by de-taping my body prematurely. And I had checked out emotionally by patting myself on the back.

I had surrendered to the pristine moment. My body was happy to concur and proceeded to shut down. I became feverish and started vomiting into the river. My nose started bleeding. Of the eight toenails I had lost, two quickly became infected. My blisters started leaking again, and my chafing areas worsened as I scratched them compulsively. Each of my legs swelled to the size of a football; my calves, ankles, and feet merged into one big blob.

I realized what I had done; I had subconsciously decided I was unworthy of feeling good about the day. I had let my guard down, sabotaging my chances. Déjà vu. Why? I wondered.

I hobbled to the medical tent.

"Hi, Mr. Cankles!" said Rob, the medic on call.

I lay on the gurney, my head shaking. My daily cocktail of anti-inflammatories were twinned with a dose of antibiotics, causing unbearable stomach pain and more vomiting. After this procedure, instead of playing Euchre or wandering around to spend time with my new friends, I angrily entered my tent. Thanks to my carelessness, I now had to put my feet up to drain the blood down to my mid-section and bring my fever down.

In the tent, my feet became permanent nesting trees for local flies, with a dozen feeding on each discharging foot. I laughed, thinking about the number of times I had pursued a fly at the cottage – one annoying, buzzing insect that had the power to ruin the moment. Now I was looking at a colony of them.

"Feed away, guys," I said.

We all have our limits and I had found mine. The tables had turned: My positive attitude was gone, small tears were flowing down my cheeks, and now I was now the one being comforted by my tent mates.

PART I
PRE-TRAINING

CHAPTER 1

A CRISIS AT WORK

I knew a man who once said,
"death smiles at us all; all a man
can do is smile back."
-FROM THE MOVIE GLADIATOR

March 2008

It was a perfect storm, a murderous tidal wave with no higher ground for refuge.

I had sensed it was coming but failed to connect the dots. Revenue was becoming increasingly soft versus the same period in 2007, and work in progress was declining as well. Almost to the day, we had enjoyed seven years of steady growth since the Internet bubble crash at the turn of the decade. I had bought a new home the year before, an act of over-optimism that in the past had always signaled the beginning of an economic correction. Whenever I felt financially secure enough to step up to a newer home or a second property, the economy faltered, reminding me it was time to tap the spending brakes.

I was working around the clock, like most leaders of a business – and I couldn't come up with any strategy other than cutting costs – fast – to save our leaky business.

As CEO and largest shareholder of one of Canada's oldest and biggest executive search firms, my job is to maximize long-term profitability. Our business model is simple: We are engaged by corporations, governments, or not-for-profits to find and attract executives to their side to help them build their businesses. As headhunters, we use storytelling techniques to draw people to us and begin a dialogue about their career. We assess them as potential candidates and start moving the right ones down a path that may influence them to leave their company and join one of our clients. We have access to opportunities that can make people's careers; as such, we are a key strategic resource to our clients. At the same time, we create headaches for non-client organizations by taking their best people away.

Our holding company owns highly cyclical firms in executive search and recruitment and staffing in various Canadian cities, and we have partners around the world to serve our clients. My partners and I have built a strong and dominant business, a work in progress with a 40-year history, almost half of which was baked before I arrived in the late 1980s. We have recruited more than 8,000 executives, more than 200 of them as presidents. Operationally, our shareholders divide accountabilities, and we run the businesses ourselves without professional management.

We make money when there are more jobs open than people searching. Such moments produce talent wars, making our services indispensable. But now the reverse was about to happen. Unemployment was rising quickly – up almost 33 percent in 2008 and going up another 18 percent before it would level out at a very unhealthy 9 percent.

Our financials followed the same curve – only down, not up. In a declining economy, the CEO's role in a business of our size – at the time with 80 employees and now, thanks to the economy, 50 – hovers between generating revenue when it is needed and aligning shareholders with a long-term view to blend and leverage diverse values, interests, commitments, lifestyles, ages, energy, and time horizons.

When business is good in a partnership-based service business, the CEO is the chief among equals. Even when the partners disagree with each other, they align for the greater good. Conversely, when business is bad, and personal income plummets, the disagreements threaten to take center stage and trump the firm's goals.

In the former scenario, business scale had allowed me to lead with the help of my partners while evolving what we offered the marketplace toward a shared vision. Now, in the latter scenario, survival instincts were overtaking the judgment of many. Given that all of the partners were commission-based agents, I had little leverage to do anything more than maintain a short-term course.

It was a real crisis. The company had gone from thriving to surviving in a few short months, and now I was embroiled in internal conversations about business direction with a group of bright and dissatisfied partners. The logical response to a downturn in the marketplace? Return to the fundamentals and focus on revenue creation and day-to-day client services, the type of activities I had last concentrated on 20 years previously. The emotional response to both market and squabbling partners? Well, as many responses as partners. Personally, I had no desire to take a back-to-basics approach. Haven't I outgrown this? I asked myself.

We did what we had to do. We got out the "shrinking business playbook" and somehow made the appropriate internal decisions, putting all long-range planning on hold while we focused on one new objective: survival.

Summer rolled in, and business worsened. Was business ever going to come back? How many people would we have to terminate?

Anxiety was now interfering with my sleep and had started to affect my day-to-day decision-making at the office.

Our business is segmented by sectors and functions, and I had embarked on running a desk earlier in the year focused on my two specialty areas of recruitment: finance was one of them and the media and marketing services industry the other. Both were now among the most dramatically affected areas of the economy.

When the markets turn this quickly, our industry's services can go from urgent to irrelevant in a New York stock exchange moment. At one point we're high on a CEO's value chain; we're on their speed dial as they seek updates on key executive hiring, hungry to locate that special executive who will help them achieve their objectives. Then, a very short time later, the markets tank, and we're lucky to get our calls returned.

While talent management is always essential, talent acquisition rapidly drops off the agenda of a short-sighted CEO who is focused on cutting jobs to save money and meet profit expectations.

Within the span of one negative quarter, a downward spiral forms: revenue is soft; new hiring is put on hold, then quickly cancelled; salaries are frozen, sometimes even rolled back; and finally layoffs are announced to resize the business to its revenue reality.

The executive search CEO job becomes worrisomely simple. We had fewer projects than we had the capacity to handle. We needed to fill the pipeline, but that was mired with conflicting issues in terms of our stated price positioning. Clients looking to engage a firm wanted different terms; given the shift in supply and demand they felt empowered to insist on a deal. Meanwhile, as search executives, we were torn between maintaining our terms for future dealings with a client and taking an assignment under different, discounted terms to generate revenue – which would set a new precedent with regard to brand, pricing, and future income.

Professionally, I had to revise our go-to-market tactics to drive short-term revenue, saying no, out of necessity, to engaging in longer-term projects. I had to stop being exclusively a CEO and run a desk like everyone else to drive overall sales. Personally, I had to earn enough to keep ahead of my own expenses, which I would ultimately fail to do.

Third Time Unlucky

The situation looked eerily familiar. This is my third time, I mused, shaking my head. This was insanity. I had been in the same role within the same organization during the market downturns of 1991 and 2001. I was 27 and 37 then, in a two-income, one-home, no-kids set-up. Life was simpler then. I was able to change course more nimbly.

Now, I had more wisdom, but I also had a more challenging set-up: one income, two homes, a wife, two young daughters, and an aging mother. And I was tired and out of new, transformative ideas, having been in the same role basically for more than 20 years.

The storm was severe and precipitous, and I started to second-guess myself for the first time ever.

By early fall, I was reaching outside my company to speak to economists, futurologists, and other resources who could point to the light at the end of the tunnel.

"They have turned the tunnel lights off," my banking friends said.

Other CEOs confessed to their inability to hold it together; they were stressed at work and at home.

"I keep my chin up and try to pretend we have a plan and we will work our way out of this," a CEO friend said. "But I have to wind myself up every morning to go to work; I am depressed and don't have a plan."

I was experiencing financial hypothermia: I knew I was freezing but lacked the will and energy to do anything about it. I had no control over the rate of decline, couldn't alter its trend, and had no way to keep our clients close.

It didn't matter what I did. "Atta boys" or stepped-up efforts to circle the wagons seemed to produce negative results.

Our business continued to decline every month. Negativity was now the order of the day. Some partners were checking out for the summer to work on activities they enjoyed. After all, their financial opportunity cost was non-existent. "Why be at work when there is no work?" or "I make hay when the sun shines" were the comments I received. They wanted to stay home when the going got tough. Some were taking time to re-evaluate whether they wanted to be in our business at all. A handful were working 25 percent harder and earning 33 percent less.

All of our revenue producers work on commission. This was a good thing in that our expense line quickly mirrored the amount of revenue we were earning, limiting our financial exposure. On the flip side, group apathy and helplessness were spreading virally.

As it would turn out, while the Canadian economy allegedly got better a year later, employment figures got worse. As a result, in January 2009, the Association of Executive Search Consultants projected a worldwide decline of 44 percent in 2009 compared with 2008, a $5 billion drop for the recruitment industry.

Just to complicate matters, as job losses increased, so did the requests I was receiving from executives in transition to meet with me, their sole purpose being to hand me their résumés and sell themselves. I was soon overtaken with 200 inbound emails a day, requests to connect on LinkedIn, and calls from job seekers.

The tables had turned; now we were the searched ones. I knew the ritual well: Talented executives come in for 45 to 60 minutes to ask for counsel and help, and ultimately, to be considered for current (unlikely) or future positions that we may be seeking to fill. When we were engaged in a search on behalf of a client, job seekers became very aggressive, vying for consideration even when the role was not a good match for them. In the absence of a match, their focus turned to asking for advice about market conditions, for ways to market themselves so they would stand out in the crowd, for feedback on their presentation styles and résumés, or for tips on job search tactics.

Depending on the openness of these executives, a courtesy interview sometimes concluded with honest feedback on what may not be working for them, as well as the hard truth about their prospects for a job, short term. Five to ten such meetings per week, half of them out of obligation, all of which were not billable. A soft form of philanthropy when it hurts to give either time or money.

A variable that caused me grave concern in late 2008 was how behind our business was in social networking, which was growing explosively as a way to connect with talent. In fact, this revolution was a possible category killer for executive search. With the advent of Facebook, MySpace, Plaxo, LinkedIn, Classmates.com, and industry-specific online marketplaces where people could find each other more easily, we were entering unknown territory. Was the business of recruitment becoming less relevant? Were we being demonized by the digital explosion?

During the previous recession, in 2002, with excess space, time, and staff, we effected a business transformation. We entered the career transition business, led by my colleague Bill Holland. The plan was to use this strategy to hedge our recruiting business and repurpose our unused space and people. Correspondingly, during 2008, and later, in 2009, NEXCareer became a healthy story within our portfolio. We assisted thousands of executives looking for work, which partly offset our losses from our core business. It also hammered home how challenging it was to look for work; few of our clients were successful in getting a job.

Another headache was my overzealous commitment to pro bono service: efforts through the business on behalf of feel-good, non-revenue-generating, not-for-profit organizations and associations. As the market decreased, the need for more creative ways to fundraise increased, requiring me to give more time and attention to the valuable causes and organizations on whose boards I sat, including The Power Plant, Canada's leading contemporary art gallery; Marketing Hall of Legends of Canada, which focused on honoring executives for lifetime marketing achievement and on mentoring future legends; and the Young President Organization, a global group dedicated to creating better leaders.

Remembering the dark days of previous recessions, I was beginning to think of checking in with a coach – maybe in December – to regroup, lick my wounds, and try to refocus and come up with new ideas. Deep down I was just hoping the storm would pass. Did I even want to be in the business? I was starting to manufacture answers, such as, It's been 20 years – should I move on? Meanwhile, less work for me as a commissioned agent meant my income would be a mere fraction of what I had earned the year before – 70 percent lower, in fact. It's tough to keep your chin up when you face a pay cut this size and think you may lose your business, too.

CHAPTER 2

A CRISIS AT HOME

*The funny thing about facing imminent
death is that it really snaps everything else
into perspective.*

−JAMES PATTERSON, AUTHOR

September 2008

My wife, Leslie, first witnessed it at the school drop-off in
September. Fees for the school year were pre-paid seven
months prior. The chatter this year was that a large number
of families were opting out of the expense of private school
for the coming year and were preparing to reassign their
kids elsewhere. (Fast forward to September 2009: When
we returned our kids to school, enrollment was down 15
percent.)

Mothers talked openly about the stress at home. Impa-
tience, arguments, and verbal fights were on the rise, as
husbands experienced unprecedented work pressures. Those
who hadn't been terminated had to do more with fewer
people, or come up with solutions to problems they had not
previously encountered. The market crash, the credit squeeze,
and a nebulous future were creating financial and emotional
pressures that few in our generation had ever experienced.

"I am trying to compartmentalize, but my work and financial stress has spilled over into the family," a friend shared

with me. "I have a debt load I can't sustain after my salary was rolled back. I think I'm going to lose my job."

I knew I faced some tough decisions at home. Our own budget was ridiculously bloated in light of thin times. I put the evil day off a little longer, however, by concentrating on the troubles at work.

We now were parting company with friends and colleagues and asked more from our staff. Salaries were frozen, some rolled back. Some people started to job share, or take a reduced workweek. Clients were asking us for considerations, sitting on their payables – our receivables. Some went bankrupt without ever paying us. Some were heading for bankruptcy while we served them and never bothered to warn us that we'd probably never be paid. They expected us to suffer alongside them.

"Hey, this is only a $50,000 fee for you," one CEO would tell me. "Suck it up; I just lost my business."

And then necessity forced me to cross the line from the business to my life.

Regardless of your habits and social standing, making serious adjustments to the way you live is not easy. I had to confront my own feelings of entitlement, of having earned it, of having paid the price. I have close friends who lost their jet, and they're still scarred by it. Deep down I thought it should have been easy for them to move on. But because the jet represents success and achievement to them, losing it represents the reverse: failure.

Perhaps I could procrastinate a bit longer on dealing with my financial plight, I thought. Instead of deciding what expenses could be cut at home, I reflected on how compartmentalized I had let my life become. My overall life scorecard was warped by too much weight on success at work. If things were going well there, I felt the wind at my back; if not, I could barely move.

I started to think about changing my own wiring; I had

put too much emphasis on revenue, profit, income, and growth. Of course, a change like this is easier said than done.

I came to realize, for the first time, that I hadn't handled big downturns gracefully. The 1990-92 recession was the catalyst of my separation from my first wife, leading to divorce. The 2001-03 recession propelled me to a new personal "best" of 210 pounds on the scale.

I needed to rework my scorecard to suit a different purpose. Earlier I had built a map of my life's priorities to help me stay true to my commitments.

My Life Map

Mother	Neighbors	Health	Environment
Wife			Money
Kids			Spirituality
Friends	My Stakeholders		Passions and Fun
Partners			Community
Staff	Stuff	Clients	Personal Development

Earlier, the map had helped me explain to my kids what my commitments were to them, and where they fit in my universe. They understood that, while I couldn't tuck them in every night, they were my first priority. It also showed them what my other commitments were, such as caring for my widowed mother and playing various roles in my community.

Now, I was going to use the map to explain why I was going to need to also spend more time at work. Ironic, considering that the exercise was meant to decrease the stranglehold of work on my life.

I stuck with the map exercise. I wanted to make sure I would focus daily on a specific positive outcome for each of the key stakeholders in my life, and on my health, my marriage, my mother, my kids, and my community. I defined a goal for each and some smaller actions I could take that would move me toward achieving the goals. In anticipation of how I was going to handle the business and its effect on our household, Leslie and I revisited our family values, which we had developed when our kids were younger. We came up with a list of values, in no order, as a way to drive our major life themes, as opposed to following a more traditional spiritual path.

Family Values

Contribution

Excellence

Adventure

Learning

Respect

Health

Love

Fun

We knew we needed to review and crystallize our guiding principles to help raise our privileged children in a period of deep financial and lifestyle uncertainty. For the first time in our family life, we were going to have to make decisions that would require a substantial adjustment on everyone's part. It would need to be explained in a kid-friendly language, linking decisions to respect, learning, contributing to each other, and maintaining family fun.

As is often done at the office, we put our new commitments on the wall at home, a visual prompt to keep us concentrating on the basics.

We created Sunday-night family meetings to discuss our respective preparation for upcoming events during the week, plan our family fun, and work in the new austerity program. All of us – including our daughters – took turns chairing the meetings. We learned a new language, with words such as "re-use," "conservation," and "contentment with what we have."

Our ambitious family project involved cutting out 25 percent of our annual spending, a budgeting exercise I hadn't done in years. It was a great lesson in how we can become prisoners of the choices we make when times seem endlessly abundant.

Not surprisingly, itemizing and debating everything was *not* a fulfilling family exercise. It created its own level of tension.

Budgeting activities that were ingrained in me as a teenager and young adult now had to be revisited. It was time to fire up the Excel spreadsheet and start the cutting. The first $100,000 decisions were painful but obvious: The Toronto Maple Leafs season tickets had to go, a $40,000 cut (yes, rail seats, but this didn't hurt too much: I am a Montréal Canadiens fan); we would become a one-car family, saving us $25,000 annually; I wouldn't be attending the annual client golf event in the Muskoka region with seaplane – another $8,000 gone; annual family trip – $7,500; gold patron at the Toronto International Film Festival – $5,000; family golf membership at the cottage – $1,500.

Other cuts were fun. No more buying wine; let's drink our own wine cellar instead of collecting (an idea we got from a neighbor in the same situation). If we needed to travel, we'd do so on points. Honey, do we really spend $3,500 a year at Starbucks? OK, let's become baristas and buy an espresso machine instead.

Others were brutal. Is this $5,000 for gardening? OK, I can learn to love gardening at that price. What – $3,000 for Christmas lights? $4,000 for your hair? $2,000 in dry cleaning? Argh. These conversations would lead us to new romantic highs – not!

A close friend would sagely advise, "If you cut out some of these small things, then you will suck the life out of your marriage; you and your wife will be doing stuff you don't want to do and it will spiral down from there."

I couldn't hear it then.

Our second big project, after cutting our budget, was to make the necessary adjustments at home. Leslie would be going back to work as an executive coach after eight years at home. Each of us would have to pitch in to ease the transition.

October 11, 2008

I got up in the middle of the night with a headache and a clenched jaw. Just like the night before, and the one before that. I walked outside and looked at the yard, half grateful for the view, half worried.

I'm 44. How did this happen? I asked myself. Feels like I should have seen this coming. I beat myself up for 20 minutes and went back to bed to try to sleep. It was pointless. In the last week, we had lost 20 percent of our stock portfolio due to the collapse of the stock market.

"Only five more years of work to make up for that loss," a friend shared with me in disgust.

Five years is not my problem right now, I told myself. If this maintains itself, it will be ten years. My burn rate was now well over my income. I was spending money I no longer made and depleting a dwindling savings account.

I wondered what we were most attached to that I could cut out right now. Our kids' private school? Our newly renovated cottage? Our house? The family skiing lifestyle in Collingwood? Our family membership at the Granite Club?

I added it all up in my head. Cutting these six items still left us with $120,000 of fixed, annual operating expenses, after tax. We hadn't cut out enough, I thought, processing the multi-tiered lifestyle that I had taken for granted. I've earned it, I protested to myself. I still want it. Do I need it? Do I even like it? I continued sparring with myself, without any definitive answers. The life of privilege that we had built now looked like a heavy load that could take me down emotionally and financially.

We were going to need another whole redesign of how we would now live, and soon. We had let things get away on us; our life was now controlling us as opposed to our controlling it.

A good money manager would say we were over-extended for my risk profile. It was time to press the reset button.

CHAPTER 3

SEARCHING FOR A BREAKTHROUGH

*A kite rises against the wind
rather than with it.*

—UNKNOWN

October 16, 2008

Our firm is part of a global executive search network called IMD. In mid-October I attended the twice-a-year conference along with 40 other colleagues who ran similar firms in various parts of the world. This time it was in beautiful Prague.

Fear was palpable at the meeting. Leading markets, such as the United States, England, and France had declined further than ours, a sign of things to likely come our way. Some Eastern European nations, especially the Czech Republic and Hungary, were in the worst shape, and negative reports were coming in from Russia. Spain's economy was in a shambles. I was shaken by the magnitude of the declines in some of our most important markets. I was struggling with a 35 percent decline, and some of my international colleagues were having a near-death experience: Their business was going down 50-90 percent.

I don't have many personal relationships with direct

Canadian competitors. Discussions with these global colleagues gave me a frame of reference on the extreme conditions we might face at home, solidifying my belief that we were heading straight for the abyss.

On the flight back, I started to prepare for a speaking engagement on talent management for the Marketing Agency Association Worldwide global conference, which was taking place in Toronto on October 20. The attendees were managing directors, presidents, and CEOs of marketing services businesses, for the most part privately held, and most were owners. I had been booked by David Ploughman, CEO of BSTREET and president of MAAW, nine months prior, a time when everything seemed perfect, when managing and recruiting talent was a top priority for CEOs. As I dusted off my materials to make some edits, I was confronted with the now irrelevance of my presentation. What had been topical in January was worthless in October.

A War Story

With the blessing of the conference organizer, I scrapped my original and instead presented a war story of how my partners and I had led our own firm in the previous two recessions, segueing into what we were going to do in this current one.

As I rewrote the presentation, I did a critical review of my decisions, key lessons, and with my leadership style when I was under duress. It became clear that each recession had left me scarred personally, the first culminating in a divorce and the second in weight gain. I also realized that when the economy was at its grimmest, it was a new vision for the business, focused on innovation and new services that had ultimately got us out of the muck, while some of our competitors were going out of business.

Equally important, I had found a way to inspire myself by participating in the creation of a project bigger than my own business in terms of its potential impact for the community.

As it turned out, conversations about that project gave me the opportunity to build relationship capital with key decision makers that would later turn into business transactions.

In effect, I was getting face time, even though my core business wasn't needed or wanted. The net effect was that we rebounded much faster when the economy finally turned. In 1991 I had co-created Skate for Kids with our founder Harold Perry and my colleague Stephen Milic, a project that enrolled 30 companies and that has since become an annual event with $800,000 in net funds raised. In 2002 I co-founded Marketing Hall of Legends (MHOL) with Jim Warrington of the American Marketing Association, which has inducted more than 50 iconic Canadians for lifetime marketing achievements. MHOL now has a multi-tiered legacy program, mentoring marketers on the rise and giving back to charities in need. Thousands of executives have attended the event and contributed their wisdom through the Mentor Exchange program. I realized that these projects were as important to me as a legacy as my core business was.

I finished my presentation with the simple statement that I needed to find a challenge, a project of some sort that could handle my sorrows.

Preparing for the conference had reminded me of how I could get out of out of the funk my business and I were in. These two initiatives had helped me accelerate the business when markets finally rebounded. I should do the same again.

At work we restructured and shelved programs, and at home we cut what we could. While it wasn't the picture I had imagined of my life at 44 years of age, so it went. Now, on a new, leaner financial diet, I needed to turn to myself and find my challenge.

Exercise is for people who can't handle drugs and alcohol.

— *LILY TOMLIN, ACTRESS*

In mid-November I slowly shifted my focus to the things I could control. I decided I was ready for a breakthrough that would help me stop feeling helpless and victimized by the economy. I decided that 2009 would end with the successful achievement of these objectives:

1. Get fit.

Why not finish 2009 the fittest I'd ever been? I asked myself. I could use the stamina to deal with business issues.

2. Change my life scorecard.

Since work had defined more of who I was than anything else, I needed a new scorecard to help me avoid getting sucked into the negative vortex of what was becoming the toughest year at work in 20 years. Work would be important but not define me. I decided to find out, in 2009, what would define me.

3. Be positive.

I decided to create affirming conversational capital to inspire myself, my staff, and the desperate people I interviewed every day.

4. Reinvent the business.

I committed to finding quiet time to partly withdraw from the day-to-day in order to focus on innovation in an industry that had gone unchanged for 40 years.

5. Help my community's less fortunate.

Being empathetic and shedding a tear was good; mobilizing to have an impact, better.

As for what would define me, instead of work, I knew it would need to be something that gave me a personal feeling of invincibility, a feeling of, "if I can do this, I can do anything." I started shopping for a year-defining project. The fitness part of my list meant it had to be of a physical nature.

The first obvious possibility was to climb Kilimanjaro, the highest mountain in Africa, along with Leslie. She and four girlfriends were scheduled to leave on January 1, ascend the 5,700-meter Tanzanian giant on the 5th, and reach the summit on the 11th, during the classic January full moon. The girls had been training since September.

I made the "ask" and was told this was a girls-only event.

Fast-forward: As it turned out, their expedition was a success; they all reached the summit and returned with a deep appreciation for Africa and its people and with the pride that can only come from preparing and making it to the top. The only snag turned out to be a nasty parasite that set up home in Leslie's liver for eight months. Her liver had been compromised, causing digestive problems, lack of energy, and weight gain. She was unaware of the cause of all this. Once the problem was diagnosed, it took her a tremendous amount of effort and discipline to rid herself of "Fred," as we all came to call it. The diet involved a heavy consumption of garlic, chlorophyll, psyllium, black walnuts, and parasite-removal pills, and cutting out the consumption of dairy, wheat, alcohol, sugars, and raw vegetables for four months. Despite this intensely difficult byproduct of her trip, one that was not atypical for African expeditions, Leslie wouldn't have had it any other way.

What about running a marathon? I wondered. No, the deteriorating nature of our business required a more extreme option: climbing Everest, going to the North Pole, crossing the ocean in a sailboat, or cycling across the U.S. Of these, Everest was the most appealing. I had read the books and watched the movies. But the cost was prohibitive, at about

$75,000, and Leslie was uncomfortable with the risks I would be taking, despite my assurances that I was worth more dead than alive. Everest also involved a full month of travel, which I deemed irresponsible.

My search for a defining experience led me back to a conversation with Norma Bastidas, who had sat next to me at a conference in Toronto earlier that fall. During a break we started talking about our extracurricular interests.

"I run ultra-marathons," she said.

"Ugh! What's that?" I replied.

"Foot races more than 250 kilometers in the least hospitable places on earth."

"People do that?"

She said it was one of the fastest-growing sports among baby boomers and that she was running in the Gobi Desert in China in June 2009 to raise money for visually impaired people – her son having this affliction. In fact, Norma, during a sabbatical, would be running seven deserts on seven continents in seven months.

Besides being shocked that people did this and somehow survived, I was intrigued by the complexity of it all. Not that I didn't believe her, but a few weeks later I had searched the Internet to see if this was real. Sure enough, there it was: the Gobi March, an open, international, unaided, 250-kilometer foot race in the Gobi Desert. The schedule calls for four approximately 40-kilometer days, then 80 kilometers on the fifth day. The sixth day is for catching up or resting, and the last day throws in a final 10 kilometers for good measure. Or, to put it another way: The event consisted of running six marathons in five days, and 10 kilometers on the final day, in untenable 45-degree-Celsius heat, in the windiest desert on earth, a mountainous area at the foot of the Himalayas climbing to 3,000 meters. It meant carrying your food, meds, clothes, and survival and sleeping gear on your back and sharing a tent with strangers. And, of course, running on sand or whatever else you came across in the desert.

The only requirements were a medical affidavit and the entrance fee.

It definitely met the ridiculous standard and I certainly wasn't typecast for it. I had never run a marathon before. In fact, I didn't really like running, nor did my body: My right knee's ACL and MCL had each been reconstructed twice, and I thought the cartilage in the same knee was partly torn.

December 8, 2008

As usual, I was going through another sleepless night. I felt depressed and thought I was losing it. All I could see coming my way was more darkness and pain.

I had been there before, but this time it was different. I had done everything I could for the business; we had had the tough conversations at home about a new lifestyle. Now I needed to look after me. I needed something to move me in a healthy direction. Anything that could alter the path I was on. I couldn't control the economy, my clients, or our revenue and was beginning to doubt myself.

Was there *anything* I could control? I wondered. The only thing I could think of came back to my physical health.

I had to stop indulging in how bad and victimized I felt. I needed to save myself from my defeatist mindset, which was paralyzing me. I needed to do everything I could to protect the business so it could weather the storm without too much damage and see the sun rise again. But that felt like having a goal to not die – how noble. I was getting depressed seeing so many people in my own and related industries unemployed and panicked about their futures. Perhaps focusing on helping the ones who were in the worst shape would give a purpose to my year and my life. Maybe I could combine that effort with my run.

Finally I thought what the heck and went online and

registered to run the Gobi March, scheduled for June 9, 2009. I paid the $3,100 entry fee in full. I had six months to prepare and become an ultra-marathon runner.

I guess as of today I am a runner, I announced to myself. I now had a plan to get myself through 2009, the year I thought I could lose it all.

PART 2

TRAINING

CHAPTER 4

THE TRAINING ROADMAP

*There is no telling how many miles you
will have to run while chasing a dream.*

-UNKNOWN

Testing, Testing

I was like many men who dismiss annual health tests. When
I turned 40, four years earlier, I hadn't had a physical since
my first job, at Procter & Gamble, 19 years before that. In
fact, I didn't even have a doctor. The big 4-0 had seemed like
the right time, so I signed up for an upgraded physical. The
electrocardiogram, taken during my stress test, resulted in a
positive: I was stopped halfway through and asked to step
off the treadmill. I was told that the result required more
investigation.

I embarked on a series of other tests. The first was the
echocardiogram, in which sound waves are sent toward the
heart and the waves' bounces are measured and collected for
assessment. The returning sound waves suggested congenital
heart disease, so I was upgraded to a third test, the Ecolite.
In this test, a radioactive liquid (Cardiolite) is injected in
the bloodstream to monitor the blood flow to the heart.
Relatively little Cardiolite accumulates in any part of the
heart where this is a blockage. Pictures can then identify the
areas not receiving the blood flow. I tested positive again.

I was confused. I had always thought of myself as being strong and healthy. Furthermore, there was no family history of heart disease. Well, not till then, anyway. Just as I was going through the tests, my dad had a heart failure and required triple by-pass surgery and subsequently a pacemaker.

Next came an MRI of my heart, which also came back positive. The next step was a more invasive procedure, an angiogram, the last procedure before surgery.

By then, in light of my dad's surprise heart problems, not only was I worried about his health for the first time, but I was also worried about mine. The angiogram, a standard procedure, involved inserting a hollow tube in my groin and advancing it through the blood vessels all the way to my heart, with a catheter at the end of it maneuvered into all parts of the heart to monitor blood flow.

The negative result of that test trumped all of the others; to this day there is no explanation for the irregularity of my heart. At last this chapter was partly closed for me.

No so for my dad. Three months later, he would die of heart failure. My mom is a strong, proud woman, but she has never been the same since Dad collapsed right in front of her. Dad's diagnosis had created an opportunity for me to have some completion conversations with him prior to his surgery, but some things were still left unsaid. As an only child, watching all of this unfold from a six-hour drive away, I raged about the hospital, the treatments, and the guidance he had been given about managing his recovery from surgery.

After signing up for the Gobi, I returned for my first physical in four years. I wanted to get to my health baseline fast. I was worried about my heart, right knee, and nutrition. I signed up for a full medical at Medcan, a fantastic private health-care clinic that generously stepped in to sponsor me. I was also granted access to Leslie Beck, their famous nutritionist. I failed the ECG, of course, but now, in light of the running, my main concern was my right knee. I had a lot of scar tissue from the ACL and MCL reconstructions 18 years prior. Flash forward: The MRI's results, which I received two weeks prior to the race, showed a partially torn meniscus that was good enough to go. I remember thinking during the procedure, at 2:30 a.m. (after a five-month wait, given that my case wasn't urgent), I realized that if I succumbed to any anxiety about my health, I would never go. Sometimes you have to trust it will all work out, I told myself.

Later in December 2008

Anybody can do just about anything with himself
that he really wants to and makes his mind to do.
We are capable of greater things than we realize.

—NORMAN VINCENT PEALE, AUTHOR

We all have a preferred learning style, and mine is visual. Beauty touches me deeply. I can spend hours looking at a mountain, the ocean, a garden, architecture, or art. I've filled my life with visual prompts of what interests me, or what my commitments are. Building on that, I converted a wall of my home office into a war-room board with the following headings for me to research:

- *Distance Chart*
- *Schedules*
- *Feet*
- *Gear*
- *Nutrition*
- *Gobi Facts*
- *Mentors*
- *Fundraising*
- *Tips and Advice*

Finding a Mentor

He who is afraid of asking is ashamed of learning.

To ground myself, I needed to research all of the facets of the project, and to get organized I needed a mentor. My wife connected me to Donna Carrigan, a 2007 Gobi participant and a certified executive coach. We met online.

"Will you be my mentor?" I wrote.

"Sure," she replied, without even asking to meet me first, a sign of the generous things to come from those connected to these kinds of events.

She collected her thoughts to help me build a plan based on her experience, providing me with key content for the war room. We set up a communication system. I reported to her by email every Sunday, giving her the distance I had run during the previous week along with my observations and questions. Her responses were always encouraging.

Her first move was to feed into my visual sense. She sent me a tiny clay pot containing Gobi sand and bearing the inscription, "From an idea, anything can grow."

To make good on Donna's advice, I looked at past competitors on the Internet, which led me to Mehmet Danis (no relation).

Mehmet, a dentist in the Canadian Military, met me at a Starbucks and shared his experience in vivid detail. He would become a beacon of hope and a close friend as he let me in on his preparations for his second desert, the Atacama Crossing, while I prepared for the Gobi.

The Race Is Half Mental

Donna's training thesis was that the race was half mental, half physical.

"Stéfan, if you can run half in training, you can run it all," she wrote me.

That's what I needed to hear. My modest distance objective was a modest 15 kilometers per week (3 x 5 km) by the end of the year; I was working toward 125 by late April 2009. (I would later learn that the race was 80 percent mental.)

Walking Counts

Another of Donna's key insights was that walking should also count as mileage since there would be times at which running was not possible during the race. All of a sudden, I was at 25 kilometers and felt better already. My first decision to focus on walking was to get rid of my car and become a commuter/walker. This added two to three kilometers a day.

Life's Enjoyment Grows with Better Health

Before the December holidays, my weekly distance was relatively low, between 25 and 30 kilometers a week, including walking. My body was adjusting well. An unexpected benefit was my performance at Monday-night hockey: I went from being a journeyman and fourth on my team in scoring to first. I had never been a "go-to" guy in hockey; apparently miracles can happen even at 45. (It does help to play in the appropriate-level garage league.)

The training was to follow the proven easy-hard marathon training rule of mixing slower and faster runs to build performance and keep things interesting. As the training continued to deliver stronger legs and increased vascular capacity, I continued to climb in the hockey standings and ended up winning the scoring championship in March. I also played tennis and realized I was chasing down balls and return shots that I used to give up on. Despite not truly enjoying the running itself, these early measurable successes in the two sports I loved made it easier for me to continue my training.

The change from being a two-way player to being the lead offensive contributor on my hockey team opened my mind to the fact that change was possible, even at my age – change that might even help me reset an abysmal business year, which was the reason for signing up in the first place; change that might even reset my life.

Picking a Theme Song

Music can change the world because
it can change people.

–BONO

When I had been having a particularly difficult time of getting motivated to exercise, during the social and alcohol-laced holiday season, Donna suggested I choose a "pick-me-up song." I thought of "Rocky" but was never fond of drinking raw eggs. I went for safety and chose "Beautiful Day" by U2, which was my Pavlovian bell, especially during the holidays, to get up and get running in the morning or to lace up my shoes and get out the door at midnight. I frequently found myself running well past midnight, after one too many cocktails. Not being a morning person, I was beginning to fall into the unproductive habit of running before my increasingly later bedtime.

Freedom Comes from Building Your Own Plan

Listen to everyone, follow no one.

–DEAN KARNAZES
(RAN 50 MARATHONS IN 50 DAYS IN 50 STATES)

I struggled to follow imposed routines and calendars and discovered that it was easier to follow a self-imposed one. Looking ahead at the March and April training schedule was overwhelming; the mileage targets were beyond anything I could conceive of doing. And the plan was for a big push in May before tapering down before the race itself. The calendar looked like this:

Day	Activity	km or time
Monday	Short run Personal training Hockey	10 km 30 minutes 60 minutes
Tuesday	Intermediate run	20 km+
Wednesday	Intermediate run	20 km+
Thursday	Rest and yoga	75 minutes
Friday	Long run	15 km+
Saturday	Intermediate run	20 km+
Sunday	Long run	25 km+
+ My ultimate May target		
December		40 km/week
January		60 km/week
February		75 km/week
March		90 km/week
April		110 km/week
May		85 km/week
June		25 km/week

Winter running included various road risks, but running in the snow was the closest I'd ever get to running in the sand.

A key component of my plan was that I would not run a marathon until the Gobi March itself. That way completing the first day – the first marathon of the race – would have even more significance for me. Another component was my decision, since I was not a runner, to leverage my other athletic endeavors as cross-training for the race. I couldn't prove that cross-training would produce a faster time, but I knew it would help me minimize injury and would hedge the monotony of training. I also decided not to run long distances in my training – all of my training sessions would need to be under two hours so I could maintain my other commitments. I kept my distances under 20 kilometers, saving my legs from a steady diet of pounding. I decided I would just have to live with the risk that my legs might be under-prepared for the challenge.

Follow Your Plan but Listen to Your Body

I built a schedule and did my best to follow it. I focused on building my capacity to do what I said I was going to do and honor my promises to myself, as opposed to listening to my body's aches and pains. Some hockey nights my training earlier in the day made me feel like I was the slowest guy on the ice.

The repetitive nature of running is fraught with risks, if you do too much, too quickly. Over time I would learn about recovery, rest, and sadly, over-training. While the science of recovery is simple and you can find an expert at every street corner, finding out what works for you and executing it is a process of trial and error. The demands of an over-scheduled and over-committed life meant I could get to the training, but not to preventative care, nutrition, good sleep, and adequate rest and periods of recovery. My head knew what to do, but my calendar had a life of its own. Fear of failure was what drove me most. I ran as much as possible, breaking the ennui with hockey, tennis, and personal training. Yoga found its way to the calendar, too, once a week.

Winning Compromises to Break Up the Routine

I quickly fell in love with not having a vehicle. I created a pick-up schedule to get me to hockey, a compromise that helped me get to know my mates better. As February rolled in, it was time to invest in a treadmill and alternate between indoor and outdoor activities. While I loved its benefits, I grew bored of running, especially on the treadmill. It pained me more, mentally, to run on the treadmill than to deal with wind or cold temperature outdoors. I got myself through by watching TV, an activity I was trying to eliminate from my life, and by listening to audio books while running outdoors.

The audio books were great. I could now torment my colleagues with the latest idea that I had heard the night before while running or walking. Looking for efficiency,

I migrated to book summaries, which yielded ideas five times a week and lengthened everyone's project list. A few of my colleagues hoped I would stop running soon.

The book summaries produced another good idea: I built a digital library of a few hundred titles and book summaries that I had heard on my runs and custom-loaded them on iPod nanos, which I gave to clients.

I'm known for being competitive, but I don't see myself as athletic. Nothing has come to me easily; I've had to work at it. I realized how little I knew about running – such as pacing, running hills, or buying the right shoe – and probably even less about everything else involved in the event, from what clothes to wear, to layering, to nutrition, to sleeping in a tent, and being forced to interact with strangers throughout the run.

Family Agreement

Leslie and I discussed what might be involved in preparing for the Gobi and she gave me her blessing without hesitation, believing that the experience would deliver what I was looking for. She also agreed to take on a disproportionate share of the daily logistics of our home. The kids had to be trotted out for music, Mandarin, tennis, hockey, swimming, and other extracurricular activities. And there was Leslie's weekly packing so we could all go skiing on weekends. We made agreements about the key daily moments I would attend with the kids: breakfast, dinner, homework, and bedtime, as well as school and activity-related events. The plan was that the Gobi preparations would occur as "no change" to them.

Part of my load was to put my own social life on hold; I'd see my friends after the race. Leslie had a busy life of her own, which included completing a demanding life-coaching certification program. We definitely underestimated the burden my race would put on her.

A Declaration

When you reach for the stars you may not quite get one,
but you won't come up with a handful of mud either.
—LEO BURNETT, AD AGENCY FOUNDER

I was signed up for the race but hadn't told anyone but my immediate family. I held back on telling everyone else (including my mother, who would worry too much) until January. I believe audacious goals are more easily achieved when written down and shared publicly. The sheer act of making it public seems to invite the universe to collaborate with you – and of course makes it difficult to back out.

When January came and I shared my news, it caused bewilderment among friends and co-workers. But they soon enough got used to the idea.

Saying Yes

Earlier, in late December, one of my closest friends, Ernie Votis, called me on my cell phone while I was running.

"What's with the huffing and puffing?" he asked.

I told him about the run and jokingly dared him to come to China with me to hang out. It took him a few seconds to say yes. Taken aback, I probed if he wanted to come to China or in fact to do the run.

"I'm going run it!" he said.

I had registered for the event after processing my circumstances and choosing to physically and emotionally immunize myself against any ill effects. How could someone simply say yes to run the desert without any consideration of what was involved? I had watched *Yes Man*, the funny movie starring Jim Carrey, and it sounded as if Ernie was re-enacting a scene that would fit the movie perfectly:

Hey Ernie, want to run in the desert?

"Yes!"

At the same time, it occurred to me that I may have been too careful and calculating through much of my life.

I figured a person making such a major decision so quickly had to have a high self-confidence quotient or be bored stiff. I think both applied to Ernie.

Ernie graduated with an MBA from Vanderbilt University in Nashville in the early 1990s. He has an adventurous, passionate personality, which he had repressed for much of his life because of his strong desire for routine. I was fascinated, when we first met, by his entrepreneurial brazenness. We became fast friends.

When he graduated from business school, he had a very successful painting business back home but wanted to be an investment banker – the legacy of watching the movie *Wall Street* when he was younger. Undeterred, he set out to research the names and backgrounds of the executives at an investment bank in New York where he wanted to work. One Monday morning, he reported to work without ever having had an interview, announcing himself merrily to the receptionist and asking for an executive he knew would be absent that week. Confused, the receptionist ultimately got someone from the executive floor to come out to meet him.

Ernie said he was reporting for his first day of work and professed great surprise that his name was nowhere to be found. The executive wasn't quite sure what to make of it. After asking for Ernie's résumé to validate his credentials, he clued in that he had been drawn into a caper by a well-researched MBA with loads of chutzpah. He told Ernie to go find a desk. There were no discussions about salary, bonuses, or benefits. Ernie smiled, accepted the offer, and started work that day.

Fast forward: Ernie left investment banking a few years later and started a merchant bank, partnering in various ventures with numerous business professionals, including his brother. Within ten years, Ernie and his brother owned various manufacturing, distribution, and retail businesses around the world and travelled to them in their own private jet.

Ernie chose to go to Gobi based on his mantra, "Life is full of small moments, good and bad." As he put it to me, "I suspect there will be moments in the Gobi I will always remember."

A couple of weeks later, Louie Santaguida, a serial entrepreneur in Toronto with a large business in environmental remediation and land development, signed up, too. He saw me at the Granite Club working out and queried what I was up to running around with sand bags on my back. For Louie, as for me, the Gobi seemed to provide a diversion to take him away from his single-minded focus on work at the expense of his family and himself. My business was imploding while his was expanding, yet we both signed up because business was consuming us emotionally and physically, 24/7. Louie was possibly the fittest person I knew. A modern-day Adonis, he looked ten years younger than his age, with a muscular frame and single-digit fat ratio. He grew up playing soccer and played for the Canadian National Junior team.

All of a sudden, I had a couple of buddies who would be sharing the experience with me.

Look Around for Inspiration

My training suffered during the first two weeks of January as I looked after the kids while Leslie was climbing Kili. But it was exciting to follow her on the Internet and to get the odd time-delayed communication. We were all incredibly proud when she and her group reached the summit. I carried that picture with me to help me soothe the tough moments of my own training that would follow.

Be a Community, Not a Team

I knew that my little community of friends who were going to race with me would come in handy for the prep work as well as on the run itself. I had been warned, however, that running as a team would put too much pressure on the relationships.

It would be easier to face obstacles alone and at one's own rhythm.

We all emailed each other – a case of the blind leading the blind. The Canadian community kept on growing. In January I heard that Rob and Katrina Follows had signed up, fresh from reaching the summit of Everest, the last of the seven summits – the highest peaks on seven continents – that they had scaled. Len Stanmore, a 57-year-old Torontonian, another seven-summits graduate, signed up, too. Counting Norma Bastidas, I either knew, or was familiar with, six other Canadians who were going.

CHAPTER 5

ASKING FOR HELP

*Aim above morality. Be not simply
good, be good for something.*
−HENRY DAVID THOREAU, AUTHOR

Possibly because the challenge was easy to understand and failure was a constant possibility, the project grabbed people's attention, making it a good medium for raising funds to help those going through tough times – which was one of my reasons for the desert run in the first place.

I considered all of the options and met with Mike Fenton, then CEO of NABS, the National Advertising Benevolent Society, which helps individuals in the marketing and communications fields get a step up in life when they face illness, injury, or employment or financial issues.

Mike shared that their caseload was up 50 percent already and that they were challenged to cope with the sudden demand for their help. NABS had helped 630 individuals and families, and had more than 1,700 individual consultations, or case interventions, on their docket. I attended a NABS allocations meeting: a biweekly round table where decisions are made whether to help a case, how to help, and with how much financial support. I was brought to tears by the courage of one of the applicants. She was facing adversity head-on, managing three jobs and a stress load of illnesses. It made running deserts look like running from floor to floor at Holt Renfrew. She, and others like her, would surely give me wings in the desert.

I presented my project, it fit their structure, and I agreed to a fundraising target of $25,000.

Asking people to sponsor me was one of the most difficult parts of the project. While I have led various fundraising efforts in the past, they typically offered donors a direct benefit, such as a dinner or an event. I needed to learn to overcome my own discomfort in asking for a personal pledge.

Fundraising

I dipped my toe into this type of fundraising by changing my email signature to include my upcoming challenge. Then I began to introduce the project. I started with friends only. I was a supplier to industry. I lacked the power of executives with direct influence over many corporate suppliers, such as buyers or senior executives of larger corporations. I also lacked their correspondingly larger network. I knew that a direct financial ask of anyone would result in a reciprocal one, for which I had insufficient funds. As such, I decided to market the project as opposed to sell it. I built a website to control my messaging and inspire donors through the use of video, which showed me running behind a truck and explaining why I was running the Gobi.

I had a few bad nights in the early going when it seemed it would be impossible to raise the funds in the worst year in memory. My fear of public embarrassment, should I fail to finish the race, was now amplified by my fear of not reaching my fundraising target.

To craft the semblance of a plan, I created a map of stakeholders covering all aspects of my life, including suppliers, clients, staff, partners, family, neighbors, friends, board colleagues, golf and ski members, and LinkedIn contacts. Then I mapped out how large each community was and then divided my $25,000 objective by target groups based on the likelihood of their support. Understanding where the money might come from gave me some peace of mind. Then I started tracking it.

NABS made sense to me because the money I raised was redirected through NABS to help white collar job seekers or financially challenged people who were experiencing high work stress. I believed it was this type of population segment that could help get the economy back on track. NABS could enable some families who lacked government safety nets to become productive again. Most NABS benefactors had demonstrated an ability to be focused and high achieving but now faced creditors who were washing their hands of them.

> *You make a living by what you get.*
> *You make a life by what you give.*
> *–UNKNOWN*

In my simplistic view, some of the individual cases put before NABS needed a helping hand, some financial bridge support, and coaching to get them back to work. After consideration, I felt we could provide the coaching support to train individuals in job-search strategies and I started to think more strategically about leveraging some of our own business assets to help NABS allocations recipients and also reward donors. In the end, we married the idea to our donors as well; we ended up also offering career advice at no cost to all of our pledgers in the form of a redeemable, transferable voucher. Being able to promise an immediate benefit made it easier to raise funds.

> *Give a man a fish; feed him for a day.*
> *Teach a man to fish; feed him for a lifetime.*
> *–LAO TZU, FOUNDER OF TAOISM*

Running the Gobi mirrored the difficulty of looking for a job, or having a stressful job. It would be the most complex emotional project I would ever take on, requiring a ton of hard work and the challenge of dealing with the loneliness of long-distance running. I would face adversity, experience self-doubt, navigate the highs and lows, and be without feedback for extended periods of time. Ultimately, I would be left humbled. But I knew this journey offered me a unique opportunity to learn about myself, an opportunity that could change the course of my life.

As business continued to slow down, I felt even more keenly my need for a mind- and body-changing challenge. I began to feel I was on the right path when a RacingThePlanet press release came out.

Pressroom

(7 January 2009, Hong Kong) – TIME magazine today named the 4 Deserts #2 on its list of Top Ten Endurance Competitions in the world. The list includes such renowned events as the Tour de France, The Dakar Rally, 24 Hours of Le Mans, Vendee Globe and the Iditarod, among others. Commenting on the selection, Mary Gadams, the Founder and CEO of RacingThePlanet, the organizer of the 4 Deserts, commented: "Thanks to all our committed staff and volunteers including the medical team for making the 4 Deserts what it is today. Thanks also to the tremendous support we get from our partners in each country/continent (China, Chile, Egypt and Antarctica). Our goal is to ensure that the 4 Deserts remains the unique international competition that it is today for decades to come."

CHAPTER 6

VARIOUS DEGREES OF PAIN

I prefer to remain in blissful ignorance of the opposition. That way I'm not frightened.

–IAN THOMPSON, RUNNER OF A 2:09 MARATHON IN
THE 1974 COMMONWEALTH GAMES

My Competitive Advantage

In one of her responses to my early weekly progress reports, Donna challenged me to come up with my competitive advantage for completing the race. I was stumped.

Half seriously, she said maybe ignorance was my competitive advantage. Little did I know how right she was. Most people tend to think in a linear fashion about a challenge like this. They wouldn't consider running six marathons plus 10 kilometers prior to running a 10K, then a half marathon, followed by a marathon, and ultimately an ultra marathon. I was skipping all of these steps. She said I could easily talk myself out of the Gobi if I had experienced how hard it was to complete shorter runs.

To keep things in perspective, it helped me to remember that my other mentor, Mehmet, placed sixth overall in Gobi 2008, just behind the world-renowned Dean Karnazes, without ever having previously run a marathon. During my preparation, I was able to follow him online as he won another desert race, the Atacama Crossing. It was a towering accomplishment that filled me with thoughts of what was possible for me. Mehmet coined the phrase "Being Unreasonable" for what he and I intended to do.

Ups and Downs

Mind is everything: Muscle;
pieces of rubber.
−PAAVO NURMI, 12-TIME OLYMPIC MEDALIST

The initial euphoric period of training yielded great results, but running itself proved an ongoing challenge as I kept increasing the distances I ran. Good thing walking counted in distance running, because sometimes that's all the soreness in my legs and hips would allow me to do. Never having been a runner, I feared that my legs, tendons, ligaments, and bones would not be able to take all the pounding. Past the excitement of the early days, yet far from the event, my physical and emotional ups and downs became a weekly, sometimes daily, matter.

Every single day was marked by various degrees of pain. The fear of not training enough haunted me, and the relentless daily training took its toll. Grimacing started from the moment I got out of bed with overnight stiffness to past the first 200 steps of my run. At times I was fueled by the triumphs of longer or faster times, but these were always followed by shorter and slower times. I ended some runs like "Rocky," arms up with pride, others in frustration and disappointment. The only constant became icing my knees.

Following a tough outing, I put up another home office whiteboard to list my reasons for running. I hoped to keep my mind from wandering.

The biggest problem was the pain. It blocked me from finding the energy to run first thing in the morning. I procrastinated, usually running in the middle of the night, outside in the snow.

Benefits of Training	Costs of Training
• I feel better after a workout/run	• I don't like it at times
• Prepare properly and mitigate the risks of failure	• Sucks up time – it seems unproductive at times
• Improved performance in other athletic activities	• Cuts in on my sleep and family time
• Personal development via listening to digital books	• Constant pain, albeit it is temporary
• See new neighborhoods	• Frequently boring
• Satisfaction of being true to my word	• I may not be able to complete the race if not trained properly
• When I pay myself with exercise, I have a greater capacity to give to others	• Denying myself all the proven benefits of running
• Potential to excel at running	• Not raising money for charity
• Could use my time for other projects	• Risk of failing
• Be righteous and say "not today!"	• Missed weight-loss opportunity!
• Not feeling dominated by the training	• Not getting the full enjoyment of the journey
• No more complaining about being sore	• Failing to follow a self-imposed program
• More partying!	• Breaking my word to myself
• Indulge in doing nothing	

Defining Success

I knew the goal. I had to focus on the objective of getting myself to the desert.

My whole life I've been preoccupied with the destination, virtually ignoring the journey. The pain I was experiencing now forced me to at least break down the destination into smaller, more realistic outcomes on the way. I chose to define success this way as my guiding principle for the Gobi March. Over time, I was able to create a scorecard, moving my focus from outcome to the process of learning and making it to the race for the experience. (In some cases the percentage of focus changed during the time from January to May).

Success Factors	In January	In May
Be my fittest	15%	15%
Be positive, inspired, inspiring	10%	10%
Find time to innovate at work	10%	10%
Help a charity	5%	10%
Make the start	10%	35%
Finish	25%	5%
Do well	20%	0%
Learn valuable lessons	5%	15%

Indulgence Is Planned

As with most diets, I needed cheat days – or weeks. Coach Donna had shared that having three weeks of indulgence for resting my body would be part of the program. I had taken one during the Kili climb, and promptly played that "out of jail" card twice in the middle months. Using up those weeks early turned out not to be such a good plan. The three weeks turned into six.

My weekly rest came in the form of a bath after long runs, seasoned with 2 kilograms of Epsom salt. The magnesium plays an important role in organizing many bodily functions, like muscle control, electrical impulses, energy production, and the elimination of harmful toxins. I hadn't had baths since I was a baby, and while soothing, I had to fight my inner voice, which insisted on telling me I was lazy.

Never Too Busy to Train

Like any over-scheduled executive, I had a large number of excuses for not having the time to train. These were often real. I had to make some creative adjustments to both my saturated work calendar and my training schedule.

My trainer at the Granite Club, Phil Delaire, designed a 30-minute cross-fit workout to simulate handling marathon-type pain, without incurring the physical stress of actually running one. After 15 minutes, I would be in some diabolically new kind of agony, but I knew I was almost done.

"Save your legs," he would call out.

Surviving 16 minutes would be the next objective to learn to handle pain longer, and in the big picture working out for 30 minutes twice a week was not that onerous.

I continued to play hockey, ski, snowboard, and play occasional squash or tennis. By engaging muscles differently than running did, these activities increased leg stability and injury prevention.

And I incorporated a few more extreme changes besides getting rid of the car.

I rearranged my office and worked standing. I became obsessed with being on my legs and wanting to know my mileage. Before long I wore a pedometer and discovered that by using a wireless headset for phone calls I could walk one to two miles a day in my office. I learned that you could burn 25 percent more calories standing versus sitting, and more if you walked. I looked at it as bonus training requiring no time away from work or family. I fell in love with it and have vowed to never sit again. I estimated that you burn close to 50 percent more calories by standing instead of sitting.

In time I also wore a backpack at work while working to train my back and legs to carry 30 pounds five to ten hours a day. While unorthodox, it made for good jabbing by my colleagues and elicited questions from visitors – giving me a promotional moment to elaborate on the cause and raise more funds.

Working Standing

*Methinks that the moment my legs began
to move, my thoughts began to flow.*

–HENRY DAVID THOREAU, AUTHOR

Working standing turned out to be a gift that I intend to practice forever. It is one of life's little treasures to which I was blind. Not only did this practice help me free-burn calories (free because it doesn't feel like exercise), it completely changed how business unfolded in my office. In fact, my new way of working resulted in five breakthroughs.

First, I found that the daily, unplanned meetings that took place in my office were far more transactional and expedient. Without an invitation to sit, everyone somehow got to the point faster. All I had to do was to be mindful of when to invite them to sit – some issues did require the kind of empathy that's given best when sitting together.

Second, I found myself far more engaged kinetically in my telephone conversations – which took up the bulk of my day – by freeing my arms and body from being in a chair. I felt more persuasive, engaged, and passionate while walking around with a headset and using my body to speak. Looking back, I think selling and presenting are really meant to be done standing, not sitting.

Third, I could stretch my back and legs easily when I was already in a standing position. In fact, after injuries, I stood on a Bosu plate to engage my shins.

Fourth, colleagues passing by could see me, which created more smiles and more impromptu drop-ins. I had always favored an open door policy; standing promoted it.

And fifth, the calories burnt meant better, deeper sleep at night, a key to preparing for the race.

My research suggested that I was able to burn 15 percent more calories a day simply by standing as opposed to sitting, and another 15 if I chose to actively walk which I did, using a pedometer to get myself to walk two to three kilometers a day in my office.

Running Games to Break the Winter Doldrums

Hills are speed work in disguise.

—FRANK SHORTER, OLYMPIC MARATHON GOLD MEDALIST

Race anyone

When out of my office, my mindset was to learn to move fast. My colleague Jeff Baldock, a certified executive coach at NEXCareer, practices his own form of race walking. He said the trick is having the objective of always passing others, by being first to the subway, the escalator, the bus, or the next street light. No longer were walks for daydreaming, coasting, or worse, strolling: The goal was to train my body to chase and reel in whoever was in front of me. I was teaching myself to move.

The Swedish way

Leave it to the Swedes to come up with ways to break monotony. Many runners practice the Swedish Fartlek approach of sprinting toward any object to amuse themselves and mix up the various segments of a run.

Runabouts

When loping past pedestrians became predictable, I started heading in a direction with no purpose but to move. Runabouts, some people call them. I simply headed in one direction until I was faced with the shame of taking a cab back – or the glory of running back and doubling the distance.

Hill repeats

I developed an alternative to stair work, running down them first and then walking up. Halfway through the training, I shifted to taking both approaches, half and half. And on a few occasions, I ran up and walked down, two, three, even five times in a row.

Elevators = Opportunity

I stopped using elevators – I took the stairs. A meeting in a downtown Toronto tower was great news, except for the part where I showed up to the meeting needing a clean shirt.

Need to go somewhere? Run

We ski in Collingwood two hours north of Toronto. My weekends were pretty energetic, and not just on the ski hills. For me, the trip to Collingwood started with a long walk and getting picked up on the way. Then, before we reached our destination, I got out, in Duntroon or Stayner, and ran the 15 to 20 kilometers still to go. On the Saturdays during these times away I ran back from the ski club to our condo. We usually left for Toronto after lunch on Sundays. I started early, running toward Toronto until Leslie and the kids caught up with me. Blizzards became my best friend: Running in blowing snow simulated desert sand and wind.

Running in the Collingwood area was not without its risks. I was forced off the road a few times and was pelted with Big Gulps by some rednecks up there. I heard "Run Forrest, Run!" more than once.

CHAPTER 7

BURDENS

*Take ANY problem in life and it will
fall under one of three categories...
Money ... Health ... or Relationships.*

–JOHN HARRICHARAN, AUTHOR

Stress

Life pre-Gobi became increasingly complex. Stress levels
soared as we tried to adjust to life with only one vehicle and
four over-programmed lives. Not exactly the picture I had for
myself, but I chose it, so I lived it. I took public transit to the
odd hockey game, sticks, bags, and all. I saw it as training.
I even opened the golf season by lugging my clubs over to the
subway station and traveling all the way to the end of the line
for a pick-up.

As expected, more stress developed between Leslie and
me as a couple. The obvious cause was my training and eventually rehab, which took me away from home during family
time and loaded the details of domestic life on her. We had
made agreements about my time. Training might account
for two hours a day and work for 60 hours a week as my
business went through hell, but nothing would be allowed
to interfere with time with our five-year-old and seven-year-
old daughters, including tucking them into bed each night.
My wife and I agreed that the two hours would come at the
expense of time between us and my time with my friends.

I tried to create a new habit of completing my training by 7:30 a.m. but was unable to break my nocturnal nature. I kept running at night, after everyone was down. Leslie couldn't sleep for worry about me as I ran the streets of Toronto well past midnight, sometimes until two or three in the morning.

The typical weekend burden on Leslie included the run to/in/back from the Collingwood condo. I was not around to tidy up and pack the kids, and invariably, despite GPS and some cell coverage, we ended up missing one another in a snowstorm on the back roads around Creemore or Stayner.

Another "burden" was my weight loss. Like all things in life, you have to be careful what you ask for. I was a scrawny six feet one inch and 165 pounds when I had been in university. But following the typical pattern of adding a pound a year or so, I was now cresting at 210 pounds. I still looked and felt healthy. I started to worry about it when I turned 40 and dialed the pounds back to 195. While Leslie added weight on purpose to carry some reserves with her to her Kilimanjaro climb, as is recommended, my training had me slimming down fast. Of course I reveled in my loss. My body changed rapidly. My daily weigh-in was akin to opening the cookie jar looking for a treat. Was it going to be a quarter, half, or a full pound loss today? I was a little too eager to share the good news. I learned the hard way not to brag – or worse, to suggest to Leslie she might want to start running too …

While I happily headed toward 168, a loss of 30 pounds, Leslie grew frustrated with her own weight. Not only had she gained weight on purpose for the climb, but the abovementioned parasite she picked up on her climb was preventing her from dropping the weight.

What was my ongoing weight to be? None of my clothes fit me. It cost me about $3,000 in alterations, not that I minded losing three sizes and re-acquainting myself with size-32 pants, my 25-year-old long-lost friends.

> *There's no such thing as*
> *bad weather, just soft people.*
>
> —BILL BOWERMAN, CO-FOUNDER, NIKE

My mileage crept up every week as I headed for the first of three peak weeks of 125 kilometers running and 25 walking before tapering down in May. I reached the peak objective during the last week of March, running outdoors in the sleet and slush and sometimes freezing weather. I had achieved the impossible.

Receiving my competitor kit from the race organizers made it real.

I was sore but elated. Poor technique, repetitive pounding, and the wrong shoes meant I had lost two toenails by that time and my now-ugly feet were suitably blistered to take on the desert.

My excited email to Donna announced I had completed the "half physical" part. For the first time, I believed I could do it, even though I knew there were limitless mishaps that could cause me to fail.

The only deficient part of my program was fundraising. My efforts were not producing the kind of results I needed. So I built a fundraising website and went on a public relations campaign with the help of my friends at Fantail Communications. They released this announcement, which got picked up in *Strategy Magazine*, *Marketing*, the *National Post*, and the *Globe and Mail*.

FOR IMMEDIATE RELEASE / March 23, 2009
ONE MAN AND A DESERT MARATHON
TO HELP OUT OF WORK MARKETING PROFESSIONALS

Mandrake/NEXCareer CEO, Stéfan Danis, Challenges the Gobi Desert and Canadians to Provide $25,000 Support to Marketers Affected by the Economic Crisis

Toronto, ON – Stéfan Danis, CEO of Mandrake and NEXCareer, is asking Canadians to pledge their support for him as he tackles the Gobi March to raise $25,000 for the National Advertising Benevolent Society (NABS), the only charitable organization in Canada that provides assistance to communication industry professionals. Further, every $100 in donation to Stefan Danis will be returned in the form of gift vouchers for NEXCareer services, a career management and outplacement services company, to pass on to someone in a career transition situation or use themselves in the future.

"I want to support an industry that is often the first in line for cost cutting and do so in a way that has the potential to give back more than the monetary value of a pledge," says Stéfan Danis. "More so than in other poor economic times, I see panic, despair, and some hopelessness in the communication industry which frequently spills over and affects family lives."

The Gobi March is the largest international sporting event in Western China boasting over 35 countries involved and travels 250 km in six days in extreme heat and wind. It is part of the 4 Deserts series which is on Time Magazine's Top 10 Endurance Competitions list. There will be about 200 competitors starting the race on June 14, 2009 of which about 30 will not finish the race. Full details can be seen at <www.4deserts.com/gobimarch/>.

Support Stéfan Danis on his mission and make a pledge online at <www.gobi4NABS.com> (since rolled into <www.running4nabs.com>) where the details of the Career Transition Offer are posted. Services can be gifted to someone recently downsized and who was not able to access outplacement coverage in any industry sector. Services can also go to a family member or a friend in the same situation.

"The hope is to deliver 500+ workshops to assist the job search of people needing direction for a job search strategy and tactics," says Danis.

The release went on to describe NABS and NEXCareer. With the help of my colleague Dijana Ebach, who hawked my list of prospective donors, I was able to get 300 people to step forward and pledge $42,000, almost twice my initial objective. Gifts ranged from $25 to $1,500, each one warming my heart. The project even caught the attention of an old friend who had disappeared and to whom I had loaned $5,000 in 2000. She contacted me and offered to pay me back after an eight-year silence. In time, I threw caution out the window, and I resorted to a few stunts, including going to a NABS fundraising black tie event dressed in my running gear with my back pack on, a good way to prompt conversations with their patrons.

CHAPTER 8

SHIN SPLINTS

There is no education like adversity.
—BENJAMIN DISRAELI, BRITISH PRIME MINISTER

April 2009

While I was on easy street, early in my training, Louie and Ernie were dealing with adversity. Ernie carried an IV with him for ten days to cure an infection, and Louie was on a first-name basis with half of Toronto's prominent physiotherapists.

April 5 was my most memorable day. Returning in the middle of the night from a run, I got Leslie up and told her I had put 140 kilometers on my feet that week, 115 of them running. An endearing event to share with anyone, don't you think? I then sent an email to Donna:

> **Done!**
> I got it done! Just came back at 2:30 a.m. and got to 75 miles. With the walking, almost 90 miles! I just went out in the worst weather – wind and sleet and rain at 12:15 a.m. – and ran a sub-9-minute 15-miler after having run 10 miles every day this week. I'm pooped but happy. Possibly it can be done! While I have a ton of self-doubt when I click on the bios of the racers – all have done marathons, ultras, or prior desert races – I've been inspired to follow fellow Canadian Mehmet Danis who won the Atacama desert race last week. Stunning that he had never run a marathon prior to running Gobi a year prior.
> Cheers, I am now going to slip into a salt bath ...
> Stéfan

Two days later, a very different story.

You don't run the desert in running shoes. With two months to go, it was time for me to sample harder-sole trail shoes. Converting to my short-listed trail shoe for the race, I injured myself badly during a 20-kilometer run, which I should have ended early. The result: debilitating shin splints, as well as acute tendinitis in both Achilles tendons.

That run turned out to be a $3,000 mistake. It required non-benefit-covered visits to chiropractors and acupuncturists; magnetic resonance, laser, active control, and massage therapists; as well as a podologist and orthopedic surgeons. I actually ran into Louie a few times, when he was getting help for his own issues. I was now seeing a specialist three times a week, mainly at the Sports Clinic, under Dr. Mohsen Kazemi, who somehow put me back together. But it took two months.

However, as in business, you must play the cards you're dealt without whining. I switched my training to the pool, first running stationary with a floatie, without touching the bottom. Later, when I had built up strength, I did the same without the floatie. Once I was able to reintroduce weight bearing, I went running in the shallow end. My training companions were the Granite Club synchronized swim team at 6 a.m., the master swimmers half an hour later, and the white-haired aqua-fit ladies at 7:30.

The Whining Scorecard

Few things are more annoying to me than people who complain, and my own level of whining was on the rise because the training was not occurring as I expected. I found myself feeling victimized. I created a whining scorecard to record my negativity and quickly became aware that I was complaining a lot. Changing ingrained habits is not easy, but the sheer act of becoming aware of this habit and writing it down made most of it almost disappear.

April was brutal emotionally. My apprehension grew. Not

only could I not walk up the stairs, but walking down them hurt even more. My hopes of doing OK were dashed. I could no longer run. Nancy Olmsted, my Granite Club physiotherapist, said it best.

"If you try to run, you may not take the start. If you rest, you may finish."

So the focus changed. Now I was aiming to make it to the starting line.

One of the amusing moments involved getting the travel visa from the Chinese embassy. I limped into the embassy and announced that I was going to the Gobi Desert for a race. They replied that the area was closed to foreigners. I argued the point, showed them race pamphlet, and they said I couldn't go. After a heated discussion, during which they got an earful, they kept my passport and suggested I return five days later to pick up the visa.

I did and they handed back my passport. Leaving the embassy triumphant, I suddenly realized that there was no visa in my passport. I walked back in and was greeted with a smile: "We told you that you can't go to the Gobi. No one is allowed there!"

I found out how to get around this. I returned a few days later and simply asked for a visa to go to Shanghai. Request granted. I had learned that less is more with the Chinese embassy.

Comic relief didn't cheer me up for long. I felt defeated; hundreds of hours of training had gone to waste. The prognosis was that my Achilles tendons and shin splints would take eight weeks to heal. There are areas in my life where I feel resigned to a certain outcome, but I had never quit, first marriage aside. Depressed, I reached out to the 4 Deserts organization to investigate postponing my visit to a future event or to get out of the race altogether.

Once you learn to quit, it becomes a habit.
–VINCENT LOMBARDI, FOOTBALL COACH

Reimbursing the donations would be embarrassing. I hoped the donors would understand it was just too much for my body.

I was about to pull the plug when a $1,500 donation from Rupert Brendon, a Canadian marketing legend and leader, came in on my BlackBerry. Rupert was neither a close friend nor client; I was shocked and humbled by the amount of the donation, and ashamed. At that moment, I realized this was no longer about me; it was much bigger. It was now about the cause. I had to go.

CHAPTER 9

GOBI SENDOFF

God determines how fast you're going to run; I can help only with the mechanics.

–BILL BOWERMAN, CO-FOUNDER OF NIKE

As I aqua ran in the pool the next day, having recommitted to my vows to run the race, my mind kept on going back to the basic question: If I *am* able to get rehabilitated in time, how am I going to run without reinjuring myself?

April and May 2009

Not being able to run shifted the focus of my coaching conversations with Donna to other areas. Between medical visits, I was now prepping logistics and visualizing every aspect of the race itself. Donna probed various components that I needed to start thinking about.

Washroom

From Donna: "Imagine 150 competitors around you as you have to go. No one cares. Many complain that it is hard to get used to during the race. What can you do to prepare yourself?"

Routines

"Consider what your morning pre-stage routine will look like in detail. When will you practice? What will your post-stage routine look like in detail? When will you practice?"

Backpack

"Learn to pack and unpack with your eyes closed. Automate everything. Choose where everything will go to lessen the frustration and confusion that comes with being exhausted and not finding what you need when you need it. Automation will save you time in the morning. Put everything in plastic bags to layer against sand."

Stare at wall exercise

"Stare at a point on the wall, such as a peephole on a door, for as long as you can. U.S. Marines can do this for 45 minutes. You will feel nauseous after ten minutes, but this exercise will enhance your mental tenacity."

Learning to run

My trainer, Phil, had attended a running clinic as he prepared to run the Canadian Ironman. With time to spare, we spent some of my training sessions analyzing videos of the clinic. Why had I never asked someone if I ran properly? I asked myself. As it turns out, millions of us just put the shoes on and go. And apparently, 70 percent of us end up at visiting a therapist.

Then we filmed my running stride for a few meters, which was all I could do, and reviewed it in slow motion, then layered it against his on his video. The differences were clear: I spent less time in the air than I needed to, which meant I was planting my feet more frequently than I should, with each foot plant compounding any possible inflammation. My poor kinetics had likely precipitated my Achilles tendon and shin splint injuries.

I let go of my fears and chose to fully believe this training was going to allow me to run pain free once I was rehabilitated. I locked in the visual of a brand new way of running and played the tape in my head to anchor it. My upper body was to be angled five to eight degrees forward to simulate the impression of falling forward and to let gravity pull me. My legs were to remain straighter to reduce bending of the knees, thus lessening stress on my already reconstructed ligaments. And I was to land flat footed with my foot under my body as opposed to in front. This meant eliminating the traditional heel-flat-toe sequence, logic being that heel striking would irritate my Achilles tendons and put undue stress on my knees, because the heel motion causes imperceptible braking every time your foot lands on the ground.

To change deeply ingrained habits is never easy. But having the leverage to change habits given my repeated failures would help me let go of the old. While I accepted the science, it didn't feel completely natural so I went searching for other authoritative viewpoints. I started posting on LinkedIn, and Pierre Saint-Laurent, an acquaintance in my network, connected me to Ray Zahab, possibly the world's greatest authority on ultra-marathon running. He is an iconic Canadian who, among other achievements, ran 111 days in a row crossing the Sahara, running an average of 70 kilometers a day. Not bad for a guy who used to smoke a pack a day.

I spent time on the phone with Ray to deconstruct the physics of running. He concurred and worked to help me visualize the movement of a metronome, akin to a scissor-like movement, each leg a relatively straight cutting blade. Then I found the story of Cliff Young on the Internet, which made me believe.

In 1983, a potato farmer entered the Westfield Sydney to Melbourne Ultra Marathon. Cliff Young was not so young at the age of 61. He had also never run a marathon before. When he showed up to run the race in overalls and gumboots, many people thought he was laughable. Running the race, Cliff's shuffling gait was outpaced by the younger and more fleet of foot runners. But when the other runners quit for the night, Cliff kept running, and running, and running. After four days of running non-stop, Cliff crossed the finish line first and set a new record for the course beating the previous record by nine hours.

Afterwards, Cliff explained to the press that whenever a
storm was approaching he would have to round up all the sheep
on his 2000 acre farm by running around after them. So during
the race he just imagined that he was rounding up sheep trying
to keep ahead of a coming storm. Today, the Young-shuffle is
used by many ultra-marathoners.

While at the podologist's, who was treating my debilitating Achilles tendinitis with two weeks to go before my
departure, I received an email confirming the result of the
knee MRI. No surprise: My right meniscus was partly torn.
I accepted the news with a smile and within an hour I was
having a glass of wine with Dr. John Cameron, the ortho-
pedic surgeon who had operated on my knee in 1991, to
show him the detailed picture. By sheer luck, we had just
moved next door to the Camerons, both of them doctors.
I was likely John's worst nightmare: an accident-prone,
former surgery patient living next door.

"You're going to go anyway?" he asked rhetorically
looking at the chart. "Here. This will help."

He filled a prescription for Naproxen, an anti-inflamma-
tory, and Omeprazole, an ulcer suppressant, to counter the
effect of Naproxen on my stomach.

I dropped a bag of food from my pack and replaced it with
the newly prescribed drugs, some Advil, and new orthotics
for my trail shoes. Over the last week, unable to run and be
gait-tested for the right shoe, I committed to the Salomon
S-Lab Trail shoes, switching from the Brooks Cascadia, the
shoe Mehmet had worn in his Atacama Crossing victory.
While I could not fault the shoe for my injury, I thought it
was bad karma not to move on. Of course the real risk was
that I would never have a chance to try *any* shoe; I simply
had to commit and hope for the best.

The week of my departure, we had a Gobi sendoff at home,
a last effort to thank donors and get new ones. The evening's

key moment was an inspiring presentation by Mehmet, who passionately described what awaited me. I wore my running gear and backpack that night as a stunt, forcing all the guests to carry the 12 kilograms on their backs and then hitting them for a few more dollars.

Then, three days later, came the tearful goodbyes at the airport.

"Be safe," Leslie said, "and come back alive!"

I walked away toward the Shanghai-bound plane, fingers and toes crossed. This was to be my first-ever flight in the oasis of first class, thanks to an upgrade, with warm face-cloths, a bed, choice wines, and gourmet food. I had never been able to justify the extraordinary incremental expense of flying business class. Doing so on this trip definitely helped start things off on a high note. I used the red wine to sedate myself, visualizing throughout the long flight a perfect story line for my race.

As the date approached, the 4 Desert race organization had been active with its marketing apparatus.

Press Release

The Gobi March (China) 2009 begins in just a few days with roughly 130 competitors from 28 countries expected to participate including a record number from mainland China. (9 June 2009, Hong Kong) – RacingThePlanet is set to stage its next event in the 4 Deserts series, the Gobi March on June 14, 2009. The far northwest extremity of China, on the border with Kyrgyzstan, in the Kizilsu Kirghiz Autonomous Prefecture situated along the ancient Silk Road, will be the setting for the Gobi March 2009, the twentieth RacingThePlanet event. The Gobi March (China) 2009 will traverse some of the most spectacular landscapes and terrain that exist in China, and competitors will also have the rare chance of visiting places where Uyghur, Tajik and Krygyz minorities reside, coming into contact with the special blend of myriad cultures and traditions unique to this ancient part of the world.

The Gobi March is known to be the most unpredictable and hostile of the 4 Deserts events with ever-changing weather and terrain including sand and dust storms, floods and extreme heat and cold. Competitors will be required to ascend 3,000 meters above sea level to Shipton's Arch (also known as "Heaven's Gate" by the locals) – a phenomenal landmark said to be the tallest natural arch in the world. It was only recently rediscovered out of obscurity by a National Geographic team in 2002.

–4 Desert Team

PART 3
THE GOBI WARM-UP

CHAPTER 10

TOURISTS ON THE RUN

I decided to go for a little run.
−*Forrest Gump*

I wish I could say I landed in Shanghai running. Given the training and the heavy workload prior to departure, plus the fact that I would be fully disconnected from the office for a full week (for first time ever) while racing, I had had no time to research what I was about to see. I just showed up and went along for the ride. I would typically have taken a cab as I do when I travel, but a group of Canadians on the same plane invited me to join them on the train and I went along. We took the Maglev (Magnetic Levitation) train into the city. My eyes nearly popped out: We were floating on the track at 415 kilometers per hour, the beginning of my Chinese-sensory-overload journey.

Urban Running

I hooked up with my friend Ernie Votis and took six days to soak up the sights. This was part of my hedging strategy; the race might prove too much for me to finish, but at least I would take home some great memories from China.

Urban running is a great way to see a city. Alison Simpson, a 25-marathon finisher, had told me before I left Toronto how she arranged her travel around marathons. She said running in a new city highlights the areas to see later. That's how we saw Shanghai and Beijing, from the unique vantage point of running through them. We ran through the Olympic nest, Tiananmen Square, the Forbidden City, the National Museum, and even on the Great Wall.

Best practices would have been to rest our legs before the race, but mine were rested from my two-month hiatus. I needed to recondition them and break in the orthotics. It was my chance to train myself in the new running style. The first day I went 5 kilometers, then 8, and then we leveled off at 10. Great news: The new stride seemed to work. My shin splints were not flaring. I was hopeful that everything would work in the desert, as well. Poor Ernie: My safe slow pace of 7 kilometers per hour meant he could keep up – by walking. I just had to run my own race without getting distracted.

While running tours now exist in many large cities, burgeoning business and hence traffic in Beijing and Shanghai cause a runner's life to hang by a thread. China's feudal system is 100 years dead and drivers are the new emperors. Pedestrians and cyclists are road-kill opportunities. Drivers here were different from the ones I've seen in Italy, India, Thailand, or even Québec. In those urban jungles, most disagreements are initiated with a honk, a cut, a hand gesture, a bump (cow bumping is a sport in India), and a few words. Here you just ran fast. Not a word is uttered until there is contact.

For the fifth day in a row, I tested my legs, this time for about 15 kilometers, in yet another memorable venue, each one being a greater cultural shock than the previous one. The Great Wall was a surprise. As you would expect, there are no flat spots, just stairs. We both had a resting heart of about 58, running it up to 165 in no time. It was soon time to stop and turn around. The wall goes on for 6,700 kilometers and probably would take us as long to get to the end as it took to build (over 2,000 years). And not all of it is maintained

– a forest of weeds and bushes seemed to have permanently set up home on the steps. I didn't think until later about the impossibility of keeping the whole thing neat and tidy.

Chinese Overload

The sensory overload of China was unlocking my creativity, helping me lock in the experience. I found energy to amuse myself and discovered blogging. I journaled the events and perceptions of my day, knowing that in a few days I might have neither the energy nor the will to do it. Despite bad habits from writing brief passages for PowerPoint presentations, and not having kept a diary since 1985 when I traveled through Europe before my first job, at Procter & Gamble, the inspiration to write wasn't lacking.

A small exhibit caught my attention on our last day in Beijing, while we were running through the National Art Museum of China. Twenty huge canvasses were displayed depicting the faces of mountain people of the Pamir plateau by a Chinese artist named Yan Yaya. Entering the exhibit I was almost hypnotized by the beauty of the people displayed and the realism and stories behind their glowing green eyes. As fate would have it, Pamir plateau is part of the Tian Shan mountain range in the Gobi Desert, where we were heading that very day.

As we headed out to the Beijing airport, I reflected that Adventure and Freedom, two of my core personal values, were being satiated. I was filled with energy and wasn't even thinking about the desert that loomed ahead. It also reminded me that while it took effort to plan and travel to exotic locations with young kids in tow, the rewards had to exceed trips such as the ones we had taken with them to Florida.

CHAPTER 11

GATEWAY TO THE GOBI

*Freedom is never more than one
generation away from extinction. We didn't
pass it to our children in the bloodstream.
It must be fought for, protected, and
handed on for them to do the same.*

—RONALD REAGAN

And so we flew from Beijing to Kashgar (Kashi), gateway to the Gobi. Louie, Ernie, and I felt a little out of place when we saw our competitors at the airport. The women, accounting for 20 percent of the entries, were positively beautiful, exuding confidence, likely from being stronger than they'd ever been. The men were buffed and radiant and were on average in their early 30s. My comrades and I had committed our first rookie mistake that day; we had checked in our luggage. When you train and all your essentials for racing are in your backpack, you don't let it out of your sight. People actually laughed at us! One participant did end up losing his gear.

The many juxtapositions within China had been evident in Shanghai and Beijing: skyscrapers within an hour of rice paddies, and steroidal capitalism and consumerism wrapped inside a Communist government, to name just two. But Kashi is different. In a country in which 93 percent of its 1.3 billion inhabitants are Hans, this city in the "autonomous" Xinjiang region at the northwestern edge of the country, close to the separated Soviet "stan" states, as well as to Pakistan and Afghanistan, is predominantly Muslim. And as timing would have it, we showed up at the height of civilian unrest. The majority of the small minority of non-Han people in China live in Xinjiang, the region is also the site of 45 nuclear bomb tests that have caused up to 190,000 deaths from malformations caused by radioactivity.

Having settled Tibetan unrest with force, the government is now turning its attention to this region to dilute its Muslim Uyghur population. Han "immigrants" are incentivized to relocate to the region. Already, this immigration strategy has yielded dividends for the government: Today the Hans own most of the larger businesses in the region. Other government strategies include restricting the time at which Uyghurs can practice their faith, curbing the teachings of their language, removing travel visas to isolate them, and sometimes relocating them.

The Chinese government refers to Uyghur nationalists as "terrorists" and has received global support for its claim. Although human rights organizations are now concerned that the Chinese government is using this "war on terror" as a pretext to repress ethnic Uyghurs – some of them branding it "genocide" – Kashi is not in Tibet, so we know little about it. The extremist reputation of some Muslim cells has meant that a few million oppressed Muslims in China aren't worth a journalist's time. This is the Chinese "contribution" to the "war on terror": a systematic ethnic cleansing of its own "autonomous" province.

We stayed at the International Hotel and were convened to the rooftop for a race and medical briefing. I got distracted by a bunch of helicopters hovering and circling a location half a kilometer away from the hotel. I went to my room, got my video camera, and started filming when I realized they were part of the government clampdown on civilian unrest. I had been so immersed in training, worrying, packing, and prepping in the weeks preceding the trip that I had not researched the history and current situation of the area. Unbeknownst to me, an entire part of the walled Old City was being bulldozed and replaced by massive marble squares, each with a Chairman Mao statue.

Kashi has 3 million citizens, and the Old City about 200,000. Shockingly, 85 percent of it is being destroyed, mostly its walled mud brick labyrinth which houses the vast majority of homes within the Old City, passed down within families for over ten generations. The expropriation, citing earthquake concerns, is in modern housing ten kilometers away from the ancestral city centre.

There's a catch when you get "the official" tour of the "official Old City": No one lives there; actors are hired to dress up as Uyghurs for six hours a day and pretend to run their own small shops selling lamps, tea, or sheepskins, all the while smiling and proudly displaying pictures of the Chinese flag.

The mood in Kashi was one of defeat and resignation, a strange backdrop for the four-hour drive into the desert. It certainly brought perspective to any thoughts I was having about the downturn my business was experiencing.

Within 15 minutes of our drive, the landscape changed to a moon-like terrain, with sand, hills, and rocks, and no sign of life. I spoke to Captain Gary Baron, COO of FLEX LNG, an offshore gas liquefaction company. I had read his blogs. Gary was returning to the Gobi to finish the race he had started but didn't complete in 2008.

"I took it for granted I could do it after having done two other desert runs races prior," he said. "I was humbled and had to abandon," he said.

Sandra Bazany-Taylor, a British woman sitting close to me, shared her insights on the race. She was only 28, and this was her third desert.

"You'll be fine. Just put one foot in front of the other."

She patiently answered my questions over the next couple of hours, after I slipped into my worry bubble.

Am I ready? What should I have done more of to prepare? Will I finish the first day? What about the whole race? How much pain will I be in? Will I fold like a cheap suitcase? Will my heart hold up? What about my ligaments? What about the meniscus? Or the shin splints? What about my Achilles tendons? How bruised will my feet get? Will I do long-term damage to my legs? What about blisters or infections? Will I be able to sleep in a tent? What about the snoring? What am I going to do when I have a bowel movement?

On and on the questions rolled. Will I tire of the food? What if people don't give me food? Will my pride get in the way of stopping if I need to in order to avoid serious injury? Will I know when to persevere? What will I learn about myself? Who will I be when it counts?

In the absence of a debating partner, my mind busied itself with creating the worst possible answers.

Just then the bus stopped.

"Bathroom break!" said the driver.

All of us, men and women, ages 22 to 59, simply walked 20 meters out into the sand, turned away, and did our business.

In these unaided desert races, you are responsible to bring and carry everything but water and a tent. Toilet paper being too bulky, I had packed wipes instead. Wipes are heavy, so I brought only ten, cut in half, for the whole trip. I redid the math in my head: OK, two wipes per outing, twice a day. I would experience, as the race progressed, a certain sense of freedom, as all self-consciousness completely disappeared in light of the bigger goal of finishing the race.

CHAPTER 12

THE LAST SUPPER

*It takes a real storm in the average
person's life to make him realize how much
worrying he has done over the squalls.*

—BRUCE BARTON, AUTHOR

Back on the bumpy road, I realized it was time to shift from being worried and embrace what was to come. I'm here now, I might as well enjoy it, I thought.

The bus stopped and it was time to get off. Five minutes later, off it roared and we were alone in the desert.

As the 135 of us walked in a single file toward the camp-site, a few hundred Kyrgyz came into focus. Being greeted in the desert by tribal men dressed up in their suits, accompanied by their families, was unexpected and beautiful.

It seemed odd that they lived here in China when Kyrgyzstan was a separate country. However, Kyrgyzia, as it was called when part of Russia, was heavily colonized and the land was given to Russian settlers, causing a revolt in 1916 that resulted in a systematic suppression of their life both before and after the Russian Revolution. Villages were torched, and many fled to China and Mongolia. In fact, the Kyrgyz ruled over the Uyghurs of Kashi for a time, partly as a result of their outstanding horse-riding skills, whether they were crossing rushing rivers, going up or down steep hills, or making their way through high mountain passes.

We were given a display of their skills as they played a type of polo game, passing the equivalent of a ball. In times past, the ball would have been a sheep's carcass, beheaded, disemboweled, soaked in cold water for 24 hours to be toughened, and sometimes filled with sand to add weight.

The rise of the Mongol empire caused more Kyrgyz to migrate to China, with over 100,000 now living in the Gobi Desert, where they are a recognized ethnic group in China. "Undying" is one of the meanings of "Kyrgyz." Running in the desert where they live would give me a firsthand understanding of what it takes to live in this inhospitable land. Their main occupation was planting a few water-fed areas, and horse or sheep breeding. They conducted the latter activity dressed in a Western style of sheepskin coat and boots.

Because of migration, conquest, inter-marriage, and assimilation, many of the Kyrgyz are of mixed origins. They have easy, beautiful smiles and distinctive features. Their dress, their eyes, and smiles transported me back to the museum exhibit in Beijing depicting the Pamir people.

The children were happy just kicking a straw leather ball. It made me think of my children. Were my daughters happy? Certainly not when we curbed their television consumption, or when our beloved dog Coco chewed on the shoes of Jade's American Girl Collection doll, Becky.

We walked toward the camp slowly, taking in the sights.

Talk about a desert storm blowing up unexpectedly: With no warning to me or anyone else, tears started streaming uncontrollably down my face. The torrential type it's not even worth trying to hide. Where did they come from? Anxiety, tiredness, or being warmly applauded for what we were about to take on? Maybe the full weight of the last six months of training was finally hitting me. I probably hadn't had a good cry since my dad died. Nice time for it to happen – in front of people I didn't know, walking in the middle of a desert.

After welcoming us, local officials formed a receiving line, which magically transformed into a group of traditional Kyrgyz dancers. Their costumes, shiny and exotic, stood out in bizarre contrast to the barren desert.

Then we were invited to our last supper of "human food." I ate next to Rob Follows, a fellow Canadian in the mergers and acquisitions business, fresh from having climbed Everest. He was there with his wife, Katrina.

"I don't intend to run it," said Rob. "I'm here to support Katrina – she's the runner. I brought some cigars, though."

Clearly there were many ways to do this race. True to himself, without real training, Rob would end up completing the Gobi March as its last finisher, walking every step; Katrina sustained an injury on day two.

Many of us opted to eat our own food, reducing the weight of our backpacks. Plus the local food put us at risk of illness from poor sanitation. I shook my head, realizing that more rookie mistakes would soon follow if I wasn't more alert.

In the valley below, Kyrgyz men, known for their outstanding horse-riding skills, were playing a game that looked like polo. Rob couldn't bear to watch – he wanted in. He missed some of the festivities, communicating with some of the men with hand motions and a smile until a toothless 70-year-old obliged and Rob got to gallop across the plain.

I learned that while Katrina had trained very hard for the race, Rob's training had been limited by an increase in M&A activity. He said he was going to rely on his determination and his walking shoes.

Soon enough it was time for Louie, Ernie, and me to meet our new tentmates.

We were assigned to tent 1 of the horseshoe-shaped village, all of them adorned with local names, ours being called Uyghurs. Tent 1 meant proximity to the finish line, directly opposite the medical tent and the open-air cyber-tent set up for racers to read emails and send one email and one blog post per day as part of a pre-paid service.

As I stepped into our tent, I tried to remember the last time I had been in one. We had just bought one for the kids and slept in it, indoors to pretend we were roughing it. The kids loved it, but I recall waking up in my bed the next day. My first and last real tenting experience was in Algonquin Park in 1996 on a canoe trip. That had proven to me that I just wasn't a camper. My idea of camping, when I was a teenager, was to sleep in my car, which I did a lot when I traveled up and down the North American coast to windsurf.

I pulled out my pillow and introduced myself to the five other runners, two Australian women and three male Brits. Most were my age, late 40s, and although this was their first 4 Desert race event, they all had a lot of ultra-marathon or desert running experience. All I remember saying was "Wow!" The karma was positive as we searched for common points of interest to settle us in and ensure that our tent mates would not become part of the adversity we would have to overcome.

My two Canadian mates and I were the rookies among this august group. I concluded that this was a good thing for us.

The Brit Trio

John Lewis (50), Andrew Kay (45), and David Breakwell (50), are all CEOs/owners of their businesses (frozen sea food, transportation, and glass manufacturing, respectively) and veteran ultra-marathon runners, John at the elite level, typically placing in the top ten in the races he runs. Together, these three have run the famed MDS (Marathon des Sables), the granddaddy of 250-kilometer desert races, the Himalayan 100-mile Trail Race, and the Raid Amazon Jungle Marathon. Details of running in leech-infested waters made running in the desert seem simple. Some of their other noteworthy adventures were climbing Mont Blanc and Kilimanjaro. In this Gobi race they were raising money for the Help for Heroes charity, which aids injured British soldiers.

The Aussie Duo

Berenice (Bez) Hines (41) is co-owner of Binbilla Wines, a successful Australian vineyard, and Sharon Richens (39) runs a physiotherapy clinic, which she owns. They were less experienced than the Brits but had completed the 96-kilometer Kokoda Challenge in Papua, New Guinea.

All of us were going to suffer, but these experienced runners would help us rookies by drawing on the unique challenges of their previous desert, forest, jungle, and mountain races. Our ignorance had been blissful; their experience was going to be useful.

After introductions, I walked the camp to spot anyone else who looked out of place. The camp was like the United Nations on a field trip:

- *There were more than 20 runners each from the United States and United Kingdom*
- *A dozen were from China, though most of them were ex-pats*
- *There were 13 Canadians, a large contingent*
- *Australia/NZ, France, South Africa, Ireland, and Italy contributed a half dozen each*
- *And Japan, Germany, India, Spain, Poland, Argentina, and Mexico contributed a few each*

It appeared the tents were clustered by country or demographics. Everyone had their country's flag glued to each piece of upper body clothing. Recalling the countries the flags represented was a real test. My last international competition had been in 1984 at the Windsurfing World Championships. I tried to recall that positive experience to settle myself down.

Just like today, I told myself, you were filled with defeating feelings of unpreparedness, inadequacy, and anxiety. And yet I had managed to keep up with the best. My affirmations proved no match for the negativity I was feeling, however. I sought refuge back in the tent where I knew two other Canadians who were equally clued out.

It was time to stop thinking and get busy, I told myself.

"Taping time?" I asked.

"Let's avoid the stress of having to do it in the morning," said the always-organized Ernie.

I started cutting out the medical Leukotape into strips. A pretty scene: I taped Ernie, he taped Louie, and Louie taped me. He showed surgical skill in taping between the marker lines, drawn around all the backpack parts touching my body: straps, pouches, and the pack itself. This was to last the week.

"You will like this, Stéf!" Louie said.

"I wonder how gorillas feel when they take the tape off Ernie," I said.

"Louie, you must be a metrosexual type," said Ernie. "You seem to subscribe to keeping your hair nice and tidy. Impressive!"

We had all trimmed our upper body, knowing we were going to cover it with the equivalent of duct tape.

"Leave nothing to chance, Louie," I said. "Tape it all – I'll take the pain of de-taping at the end of the race over getting chafed during it."

"Not known for a high tolerance to pain, Stéf?" Ernie asked.

I was half mummified – my back, deltoids, shoulders, chest, and abdomen provoked laughter, which would continue for the whole week.

"Hey, maybe I don't need a shirt!" I said. "Could we embroider the flag on the tape?"

We found out the next day that the three of us were

among the few who had taped proactively, and it turned out to be a good move. If you forgot to tape, or taped too late after feeling a hot spot, the chafing that resulted was vicious. Taping our feet – heel, ball, and each toe – was a daily ritual that itself took almost an hour.

Trying to delay the inevitable, we stayed up past most of our camp mates and had our last supper outside.

It seemed the right time for a speech.

"Guys, thanks for coming and I hope this turns out the way you hope," I said. "It means a lot to me that you're here and I look forward to sharing this experience with you."

After a while Louie blurted it out, "What have we done?"

We fell silent. By now we were the last ones up, taking in the lunar landscape. I gazed in wonder at the shiniest stars I had ever seen.

Finally, Louie said, "I want to pace myself – I'm not sure my Achilles have healed."

"Dunno – I guess we'll pace ourselves," said Ernie.

"I struggle with pacing and usually go out hard and typically finish slow," I said. "But the odd time I sneak in a burst at the end,"

We agreed that our major objective was simply to finish, though preferably not last.

"I'm sure we'll speak tomorrow," I said, "but knowing me, I'll get to the start line with no time to spare and I'll bolt out until I need to slow down. So let me say it now: best of luck, guys."

Being a light sleeper, I dreaded going to bed. I inserted my earplugs, put my eye covers on, and popped a sleeping pill – a ritual that would bring laughter to everyone in the tent. Then I lay in bed wide awake for most of the night, running a tape in my head of how to run. I heard trainer Phil's voice telling me, "Land flat footed. Don't heel strike. Lean five degrees forward to let gravity pull you. Your legs are scissors. Don't kick out – save your knees and shins."

While the others snored, I decided to check my food rationing for day one. I would intake the following while running, to be repeated during each 10-kilometer leg:

- *Two soluble electrolyte pills to be put in my 750 ml water bottles at every checkpoint*
- *One half of a 50 mg Extra Strength Advil (if needed)*
- *A 28 g bag of Jelly Belly Sport Beans, one electrolyte bean to be consumed every five minutes*
- *One salted almond every 10 to 15 minutes, from a small bag containing 30 for the day*
- *A small beef jerky stick*
- *One power gel for the day, to be used on a sugar-need basis, likely during the last 10 kilometers*

I could check for all these easily, even in the dark. At Donna's recommendation I had rehearsed this procedure with my eyes closed.

The plan was to consume my rations while running, whether I was hungry or not. The rations were designed to help me retain water, give me a caloric punch, be somewhat tasty, and add a layer of anti-inflammation to my daily intake of Naproxen. The rest of the food was sealed away and rationed in pouches for each of the five days. This kept me from consuming the next day's food, which would have been a catastrophe.

I ventured out for my first pee. For most of the following nights, once the camp was set up higher in the Tian Shans, I would learn to perform this task in my sleeping bag using a cut-up plastic bottle.

PART 4
THE GOBI RUN

CHAPTER 13

DAY ONE: ELATION

We are different, in essence, from other men. If you want to win something, run 100 meters. If you want to experience something, run a marathon.
—EMIL ZATOPEK, OLYMPIC MARATHON WINNER

June 14

Up early and fidgety, I looked around and tried to pay attention to what my more experienced ultra-marathon tentmates were doing, unsure whether the routine I was committed to was the right one. I ate my first half meal before the organizers briefed us. Conditions were ideal for a first marathon, they said, spelling it out for us:

- *1,675 meters of altitude and climbing*
- *Forecast of 44 degrees Celsius*
- *The course will have water crossing*
- *A third riverbed, rock running*
- *Serrated mountain crossing*
- *Lots of sharp sand dunes in the back half*
- *Village finish 42 kilometers away*

I remembered what Mehmet had told me about the rocks: "Keep your head down; concentrate, and plan every foot

plant. Roll with them. You could twist your ankle in the first
ten minutes if you're not careful."

We're Off!

At 9 a.m., with a 120 heartbeat, in front of ten spectators
(all volunteers), and after the proverbial "10-9-8-7-6-5-4-3-
2-1, go," off we went, 135 runners screaming. I bolted out,
adrenaline pumping. Within 500 meters, Louie, Ernie, and I
had separated. After calming myself down, I found Ernie and
ran with him.

During the first kilometer we were in a beautiful, deep,
shaded riverbed beside a gushing river. Just what Mehmet
had described. I found it impossible to pace myself and to
fully appreciate the beauty around me; each step required
complete focus. Some runners thrived and were at one with
it; others had to slow down to a walk/hop. Each loose baseball-sized stone could end your race. We no longer looked at
the horizon; we were forced to look down.

We got to the first river crossing and I had to decide what
to do: venture in or try stopping to wrap thick garbage bags
around my feet to keep them dry. I chose the latter. I promptly
fell into the river, and while sitting in it, removed my shoes.
The decision had been made for me. The leather of our shoes
rapidly expanded, and our feet, which were now drenched,
started sliding inside them and within 40 minutes of the race,
the blistering started .

Ernie's body language at the first crossing said it all. He
hadn't gotten his head around the fact that a river was the
first obstacle. He was upset.

"This is silly," he said.

"Not quite Central Park, hey?" I replied.

We had both spent countless hours visualizing what the
race was going to be like but somehow hadn't focused on
how we would react to a real river and loose stones. I had
been told about the rolling rocks but hadn't created a mental
strategy for coping with them.

One part of me was convinced there couldn't be any more surprises; the wiser part knew there would be many.

I had a profound moment in the first 30 minutes of the race as I watched Ernie and the field. I sensed that many weren't going to finish the race. I decided that I would welcome anything that was unexpected and befriend it and preferably laugh about it out loud. I remembered a speaker's description of how she carried a magic wand in her office; when issues arose, she shooshed them away. I laughed and chose that approach. If ignorance had been my asset before, adversity would be it now. Many of the runners were cursing; I chose to feel that life was perfect the way it was and started laughing. I learned quickly that if you allowed a large black cloud to follow you around in the desert, you would perish rapidly (although the shade sure would have been nice).

I found out later that I was re-wiring my brain by putting powerful and positive interpretations on unwanted or unforeseen stress. The rocks and river were a negative event to most of the runners, and their performance fell in step with their mindset, slowing them down. I was converting adversity into an advantage. My attitude had me floating from rock to rock. I started to accelerate. Bring it on, I thought. Ernie and I ran side-by-side.

It is not the strongest of the species that survives,
nor the most intelligent that survives. It is the one
that is the most adaptable to change.
–Charles Darwin, naturalist

We hit the first 10-kilometer checkpoint and re-filled our two 750-milliliter water bottles. In this race format, we were entitled to 1.5 liters of water every 10 kilometers (at three daily checkpoints) and 3 liters of water at the end of the race to last us for recovery, dinner, overnight, and breakfast. That came to 7.5 liters of water per day.

I still had water left in my bottles when I hit checkpoint 1 and was berated for it. I learned that I needed to fully hydrate and drink my entire allotment to avoid suffering a few hours later. Long-distance running is unforgiving: By the time you realize you have under-hydrated, your race may just be over.

Marathoning is like cutting yourself unexpectedly.
You dip into the pain so gradually that the damage
is done before you are aware of it. Unfortunately,
when awareness comes, it is excruciating.

–JOHN FARRINGTON, OLYMPIC MARATHONER

My pre-determined checkpoint system was to insert soluble electrolytes in each bottle, pop one Advil, and get right back to running. Some competitors hung around the checkpoint and even sat for a while. I was afraid my body would stiffen up, and just wanted to keep my momentum.

I found a spot to pee, and we continued to move along. We had not communicated formally about our individual or mutual objectives. It became clear that we weren't on the same page – that we had different expectations. While my stated objective was to finish, my competitive wiring had me focused on moving as fast as I could. Ernie, in contrast, had signed up for the Gobi looking for adventure. Tension was building. Later he would tell me he was pissed at me for not being clear about my expectations. "Then, just before the second checkpoint, I started to get upset with myself," he said, "thinking I should have known better and prepared accordingly."

The silence was deafening. After the second checkpoint, he peed and I continued to move, running slowly to allow him to catch up but fast enough to not lose valuable time. I hadn't noticed that he had waited for me earlier. He caught up and ran past me, he with unlimited speed. I caught up to him, panting.

"Are you racing?" he asked.

"Yes. This is my first marathon; I'm going to give her all I've got," I said.

"I can't believe it."

Our completely different expectations were now obvious to us. I had thought that he had been frustrated at not being able to establish a pace the way a three-hour marathoner can, because he had to rock hop and cross a river ten times instead of running.

After pitting for water at the second checkpoint, I was thrilled to see that I was in 31st place – an unexpected result for my first 20 kilometers in two months.

Ernie and I looked at each other and exchanged a few words. Intuitively, I realized there was nothing to do but apologize and leave. I wanted my first marathon to be the best it could be, which meant dismissing what had just happened and focusing on getting to the finish line as quickly as possible.

A few minutes later, Ernie, running alone, was fiddling with his iPod and came across a banked section with a boulder at the top. He chose the path of least resistance and jumped on it as opposed to going around it. It moved and he twisted his knee. Our misunderstanding and his mood would ultimately cost him the race.

It was time to meet people. I started to catch up to people, introducing myself, finding out a bit about them, and then moving forward to the next, building my community, one person at a time. I caught up to David Pearse (50), a towering giant from South Africa who ran next to petite Diana Hogan-Murphy (31), from Ireland. They ran together despite not being eligible for the 4 Desert team competition, which required at least three for a team. They had met during a New York marathon and continued their friendship, running London and Paris together. Diana escalated their adventure to running the Marathon des Sables in 2008.

David said that, the night before the start of the Marathon

des Sables, they had decided to run together and did so supporting each other for seven days with great success. This led to their running a famous European race called Trans-Alpine as an official team. They signed up for Gobi in late 2008 and met up for a week in South Africa to train and run the Comrades Ultra. As it would turn out, at the end of the first day of this Gobi race, Diana unexpectedly led all women and Dave had to adjust to an unanticipated role: being a member of a duo and thinking about the other person's victory.

Getting to Know You

Later, I ran alongside a team of three Americans, who were raising money to fight lung cancer. They were feuding; one of the guys wasn't having a good day and wasn't keeping pace. We talked while running but the bad karma soon prompted me to move on. That night, this team imploded, and from that point they ran on their own; switching mid-stream like this during was allowable in the Gobi race format albeit with an added time penalty. The three of them were superb runners and would have easily won the team competition had they stuck together.

After 25 kilometers we emerged from the riverbed and ran through spectacular, jagged, needle-like mountains that looked like Wonder Mountain at Canada's Wonderland amusement park north of Toronto. We popped out on a plateau in front of the Tian Shan mountain range that reached 7,400 meters at its highest point. I got goose bumps; we hadn't been able to see the peaks until we came out of the canyon.

I ran for a while with John Carter (27), an investment banker at Fortis who lived in Hong Kong.

"I've had to forego my entire social life in order to be here," he told me. "I've been running 100 to 160 kilometers a week in hilly Kowloon and working 15 hours a day."

His ill grandfather had provided the inspiration, and John

was going to push himself to his limits. The Gobi run also marked his transition to a new life; he was leaving Hong Kong to ultimately go back to school for an MBA. Over the next few days, I met many others who were embarking on a new journey, or hitting a milestone of sorts.

I stay glued to John. We talked about our love of skiing for a while. All I could think about was holding on to him for dear life, knowing that keeping pace with a runner of his caliber would result in a great finish for me.

The terrain had sharply undulating hills, 30 meters at a time, 10 of them in a row. You ran-walked to the top, putting your heart into the red zone, and then negotiated a run or slide down the underside. There was never a flat spot.

When we passed the last checkpoint at 30 kilometers, I realized a miracle was in the making. I wasn't 31st after all; that was my bib number. John and I were in 12th and 13th place. We agreed to push. He wanted a top ten finish, highly motivated by the list of people ahead of us, particularly the fact that his buddy Eric LaHaie was in the lead overall. I started thinking about lucky Chinese numbers eight and nine and agreed to pay the price and go for broke. I might as well make today the best running day of my life, I thought, which it was anyway because it was my first marathon ever. I'll deal with tomorrow when it comes.

I then realized that, for me, going fast required collaboration with a competitor to push each other and work as a team against the field. There we were in the 45-degree heat, with John doing the pacing and me the huffing and puffing but cheering him from the back. We reeled in four runners during the last 10 kilometers.

With 5 kilometers to go and in the clear with everybody behind us, I felt a shock pulsing in my left shin. We stopped and looked down, bewildered, at my convulsing leg. I had never had that sensation before. It passed after I lay down in the dirt for a couple of minutes.

With only a kilometer left, I invited John to go on his own. We were now entering a village and I wanted to savor the last stretch alone. I stopped and hugged some beautiful kids, who were cheering us on.

I extended a hand and they took it. We ran together to the finish. I kept on repeating "Canada," and they started chanting it back. We crossed the line together, high-fiving (I had to teach them how). I felt like Angelina Jolie at an adoption center. It was a moment of pure joy.

I sat down in the finish-line tent in shock. It was one of the happiest moments of my life. My first marathon time was five hours and eight minutes, slow for a marathon but fast in these adverse conditions and good enough for a lucky #9 finish overall. I was the second Canadian, with Kevin Lepsoe (29) ahead of me. Kevin is a banker based in Hong Kong who was redoing the Gobi after injuring himself the previous year while running it. He said he had been looking for a memorable achievement "of great difficulty," as he termed it, before crossing into his next decade.

My joy was temporarily punctured when I realized how one stupid injury could ruin everything. Kevin had slipped from 16th on the first day in 2008 to 80th. He had trained very hard for Gobi 2009. A little divine justice and a lot of hard work had him in sixth place on the first day.

The American team rolled in, and then the Diana and David duo 10 to 15 minutes later, followed by my Canadian buddy Louie and shortly thereafter Ernie.

In what would become a ritual at the end of each day, I walked over to our tent to find John Lewis, who had been there for at least 30 minutes and was lying down, his feet up to drain blood back to his thumping heart.

"Hey mate, good run!" he said, as he did every time.

That night I went to the cyber-tent for my allotment of sending one email and one blog post. I blogged happily for anyone who was following my progress. I wanted to build memories for myself and the words seemed to flow freely, despite my aches and pains. Early results had been posted on the Web and my family would know I had crossed the finish line and completed my first marathon ever. I got my first emails, all of them best wishes sent prior to today's race, including some from the family, which at one and the same time made me teary and gave me an amazing lift. Communication was a day delayed; I wouldn't see comments on my first day until 24 hours later.

I bounced between disbelief and joy over what I had achieved. All fear of what lay ahead was gone.

When Norma Bastidas, who had first mentioned the race to me in September, ran across the finish line that day we congratulated each other and felt that emotional moment runners around the globe share at the end of a race. She was second overall among women and I was first in my 40 to 50 age group, with a 15-minute lead on none other than Louie.

"Stéfan, you are in control of the 40 to 49 age category sub race," she said. "You will win this!"

It was like being told at the 14th hole that you were having a great round of golf. Instead of thanking her for her encouragement, I replaced the joys of the day with the fear that I couldn't hold on. Fraudulent thoughts like "I don't belong there" and "You're not a runner; you wait and see" reverberated in my head. I had hoped just to finish, never thinking about doing well.

I retreated for a conversation with myself. I had always known that I was afraid of failure – I had worked hard to negate its debilitating effects. Now, for the first time in my life, at the ripe old age of 45, I understood that I was also afraid of success.

Never having run seriously before, I had never even thought of myself as a runner. I expected to do poorly. When friends asked about the race, I slid in that I wasn't a runner, pitying myself as the victim of injuries, or old age, protecting myself from any expectation that I would have to live up to. Now I realized that it was time to accept that I had done the best in my training that I could. I would have to see the results of it now, on the race itself, when it really counted. It was time to let go of the destructive "not good enough": no more hiding! I was first in my age group and it was time to step up and see what might happen while refusing to layer expectations on myself.

The desert was becoming my teacher. I shook my head in disbelief at the whole thing and laughed out loud.

I would find out that we all had our issues.

Norma, a charismatic and stunning black-haired Mexican living in Calgary, was a case in point. She said running deserts helped her gain her own acceptance and step into the power of her own beauty.

"I like myself a lot more now," she said. "I have struggled with self-image for as long as I can remember, growing up in a beauty-obsessed Latin society. And ever since I started running desert races, I am content with just being me."

Her awakening did not come easily.

"The biggest price I had to pay was losing relationships. Ultra training takes a long time and focus, and life goes on. The people close to you sometimes end up going in different directions. Being a single parent, I had to learn to be even more efficient with my time. But the human body and human spirit are capable of a lot more than we ever give ourselves the opportunity to discover. Every time you overcome a challenge, the boundaries of what's possible expand dramatically."

Ernie came in among the top 20 and shared that he was banged up and his knee felt weak. His spirits were fine but he had found no beauty in the first day. I felt uncomfortable being ahead of him; the order of things seemed upside down.

Camp was in a village. The local Kyrgyz generously vacated their homes so we could have a roof over our heads.

We shared the war stories of the first day, the rolling rocks, river crossings, Tian Shan mountains, the village children, and 44-degree-Celsius heat.

Although blisters were developing, our backpacks were already getting a little lighter as we ate a dinner and a breakfast pouch. I marveled at how tasty the soupy dehydrated food was. With not much else to do, I celebrated each spoonful as if it was my last. Each day I amused myself thinking of the feast ahead of me. Would it be beef stroganoff or chicken tikka?

A special relationship was developing among our tentmates (albeit we were in a house that one night). The reasons why they were here were fascinating.

Bez said she ran to model hunger to her kids who have been raised in affluence. She said she wanted them to learn that rewards come from hard work, dedication, and sticking with it.

Sharon said she benefited from stepping off her island to meet people from around the world. She felt that although she lived far from other continents, it comforted her to know that the issues we all faced were universal. As a therapist, she was also fascinated with the body and mind connection that this event could provide.

The British guys were doing one such event together once a year to step out of their comfort zones and step away from the trappings of life.

As day one ended, I felt I needed to be gracious and suppress my happiness, given Ernie's pain and disappointment. I was still numb about what had happened between us out there in the canyon.

I went to the cyber-tent. Emails were starting to flow in from back home.

email
Rooting for you Stéf! Good luck as you step into the land of the unpredictable. No doubt you'll have amazing stories to tell of obstacles

you had to overcome but couldn't foresee before starting the race. We know you're well prepared, mentally tough and flexible in your thinking … all good things as you embark on this adventure. We're with you 200% and looking forward to celebrating. Congrats, getting to the starting line is a huge accomplishment. We are so very proud of you! Tracey Sutherland

CHAPTER 14

DAY TWO:
RUNNING ON MARS

*You have to forget your last marathon
before you try another. Your mind can't
know what's coming.*

—FRANK SHORTER, OLYMPIC MARATHON WINNER

June 15

Ignorance was no longer my main advantage. Stiff as a plank, I came to on day two thinking there was no way I could get back out there. I indulged the thought of staying in my sleeping bag, laughed, and got on with my preparations.

The morning routine was textbook for me, designed after listening to Mehmet Danis describe his experience. Dress up, but wear sandals, eat half of your morning meal quickly, visit the latrines and hope for the best, pack your bags, stretch, and finish your meal while listening to the daily briefing. Allow 45 minutes for draining your refilled blisters, cutting your nails, and re-taping your feet.

Having done well on day one, I talked to Ernie and we agreed we would split up. He was in pain and unsure how he would handle the terrain. I decided again to defy marathon wisdom to control speed in the first half and push in the back half. I followed my modus operandi of going hard early to see how long I would last. I had never run two long distances on consecutive days before. The most I had run, back to back during training, were two half marathons.

The briefing was clear:

- *Steady climb out of the village*
- *Running on Mars-like terrain*
- *Massive dune running*
- *Finish in clay labyrinth*
- *Temperature rising to 45 degrees*
- *Camp finish at 1,820 meters 42 kilometers away*

A Legacy of Big Thighs

We left the village and it was all uphill over a mountain range. I found John Carter again and lashed myself to his mast for good fortune. This stage was aptly named Mars, with 200- to 300-foot rolling clay dunes to run over. The landscape, wind-swept into angular and shapely mounds, was hypnotic. I had never seen such beautifully intense color variants: vibrant shades of ochre, garnet, crimson, orange, brick, and blood.

Ten minutes into the day, my legs were on fire and I laughed my way through, thanking my mother for giving me strong thighs. As a kid I had cursed them because kids used to laugh at me for their disproportionate size. I marveled at the distinctive shapes of the dunes. John and I were again in the top 12 by the halfway mark. I started to dream this was going to be another miracle.

Shortly out of the second checkpoint, somebody spotted the nationality patch on my arm and yelled out, "Hey, Canada!" I turned back and saw Ludvig Landgren from Sweden, who yelled, "I have your solar panel, your sleeping bag, and your medical kit; you are losing your gear – your pack is ripped."

Unbeknownst to me, my stuff had been falling out for the last fifty meters or so. As I went back to pick up the yard sale, my pack fully opened and the rest of my gear scattered. I boiled into a rage, my adversity lessons of the day before quickly forgotten. I guess adversity was OK for the field, but for me alone? It made for an odd moment, as three competitive guys considered the misfortune pertaining to one. I stewed; John assessed the situation, pitched in, wished me luck, and left; and Ludvig stayed longer to help. His generosity touched me. Ten minutes later, back on our way, I tried to pay him back by pacing him. I was still angry and almost put an end to my race by falling and twisting my ankle. Somehow I got lucky and it was fine.

We spoke the whole way as we ran. He was clearly ambitious. He had run the Great Wall marathon earlier in the year where runners actually race on parts of the wall that Ernie and I had run on the week prior. He was also climbing the ladder rapidly as a 35-year-old executive at Ericsson China. He shared that he was running to learn more about himself and expand his capacity to grow as a person. To me, he was already the picture of a perfect gentleman. Interestingly, his generous way with me ended up touching him as well.

"I realized the impact of comradeship when I helped you and saw how moved you were," he would say later. "It made a very lasting impression on both of us. Who cares if you lose time by helping someone out when instead you make lasting friendships out of it?"

After 45 minutes I couldn't keep up the pace upfront.

"Time to let you go," I told Ludvig.

Ludvig passed me. I tried to follow, but lost him. I decided to change my mood by listening to my U2 theme song. I forced myself to associate a good, happy, "grateful to be alive" mood to what was happening. It worked. But I noticed that my pace had slowed down; while the music made time go by quickly, it had also lulled me into a more leisurely pace.

Louie caught up with me while I was pitting at the last checkpoint. He and I had experienced similar breakdowns while training and we were both rookies. Seeing him awakened my competitive spirit and gave me a surge of inspiration to go after Ludvig. It felt odd to be going on a chase as opposed to waiting for my friend, but I was operating on pure instinct. With renewed energy, I caught up to Ludvig and passed him on the steep uphill, and then started a huge descent on a dirt road until it was time to enter the soft clay hills where the sand submerged my feet for a few hundred meters, each step more maddening than the previous.

Disoriented

I was now running toward the bottom of a sizzling hot and narrow clay labyrinth. With no wind, the temperature soared above 45 degrees Celsius. The footpath at the bottom, a dry packed riverbed, was twisty, a meter wide, with walls that were 30 meters tall.

I was disoriented and fatigued and ran out of water and food. Because of constant turning in this running maze, I could feel my feet tearing apart. We had been advised to stop, take our shoes off, and re-tape our feet at the first sign of a "hot" spot: the sensation you get before your feet blister for good. The idea was to prevent blisters from spreading or cutting the flesh deeper. My mind tricked me into thinking we must be close to the finish because I had run out of food and water. I listened to my mind but not my body and continued.

Even with the numbing effects of the anti-inflammatories and Advil, I had never suffered pain like this. Down deep I knew I was experiencing only a fraction of what it was going to feel like later as my feet continued to shred. I became feverish and dehydrated and started dry heaving. My head wanted to explode. Occasionally, I hit my shoulder on the clay walls, which at least helped to keep me awake. I tried to stay calm and progress slowly toward the finish.

*The man who can drive himself further once
the effort gets painful is the man who will win.*
–Sir Roger Bannister, First Man to run a sub-4-minute mile

Forty minutes later, I came groggily out of the canyon. I saw the camera crew and ran toward them as if they were the infirmary. I could hear the camp's music. My blisters were screaming by then. I was disoriented, running toward the music but off course. Ludvig came out two minutes later and headed correctly to the finish in front of me. Poetic justice, since he had helped me two hours earlier. I collapsed when I crossed the finish, face in the dirt.

Recovering

When I got up, Louie was rolling in, just a few minutes behind. We hugged and helped each other to the tent where John was in his usual position, feet up. Thirty minutes later, Andy, another Brit, rolled into the tent. He was in bad shape, totally disoriented. He slugged down a recovery mix and puked it all over me. I chose to laugh about it. I used alcohol swabs to clean myself up. Hygiene was becoming an issue. A virus was spreading in camp; people were already getting sick and infected.

"Why are you doing this to yourselves, guys?" I asked.

David Breakwell answered: "I guess we had a cumulative mid-life crisis when we turned 40 a decade ago; our businesses were well established and work seemed less of a challenge."

David said he didn't want to sound pretentious but that "financially we had pretty much all got our stalls set up. We all needed something to get the juices going. These races are billed as the toughest foot races on earth and we thought, Why not start at the top? We just went for it."

Some got on gurneys and were given antibiotic cocktails with defined intra-venous drip intervals. They were required to write each interval and dosage on their arm. Luckily, I wasn't one of them.

That night I realized I needed to expand my definition of adversity. There was what we all faced, and there were the individual trials each of us faced separately. I searched for other mental tactics to avoid succumbing to a disempowering mood change. I had rolled my ankle that day purely out of lack of concentration, indulging my bad mood instead of being alert to the terrain. Was I like this at work? Was I the kind of leader people avoided asking a question if I was having a bad day? What about the other parts of my life? Do I amplify the little obstacles I face, making mountains out of molehills?

It took all the discipline I could muster to keep from wallowing in my physical and emotional breakdowns. We were in unimaginable pain, and most of us didn't know how to handle it. It was humbling to see successful people brought to their knees and sometimes to tears. I was one of them. I kept closing my eyes and telling myself to stop whining: I was here by choice.

The pain and tiredness made it difficult for everyone to filter their emotions. By now bedside manners had been tossed to the winds. Were we becoming more authentic by skipping the niceties?

I headed over to one of the communal roundtables for dinner to sample another bag of dehydrated food. There was a fairly large contingent of French nationals, including a couple celebrating their tenth wedding anniversary.

"Cyril and I want to reconnect and do this adventure together," said Valerie Autissier.

They made every step together until Cyril was injured on day four.

It had been 12 hours since the day's race had begun and still no sign of Ernie. I was worried that he was baking in the sun, doing irreparable harm to his knee, and out of food for the day. I was on a vigil, waiting for him at the finish line. After a few bongo drum alerts, drumming in other competitors in various states of agony, Ernie finally heaved into view. He was invited to step into the sweeper, the all-wheel vehicle, for the last part of the race, but declined and eventually hobbled over the finish line. He insisted on completing the race he had started that day. He had endured untold amounts of pain and wanted to end it in his own terms.

By then, many of us were waiting for him. His struggles would provide the glue for our tent to stick together and elevate our level of care for each other so we wouldn't lose another mate. What he did was heroic.

Running is not, as it so often seems, only about what you did in your last race or about how many miles you ran last week. It is, in a much more important way, about community, about appreciating all the miles run by other runners, too.

-RICHARD O'BRIEN

There would be no more running for him in this competition. After hundreds of hours of training and thousands of dollars in expenses, his race was over.

"Not finishing is one of my greatest failures ever," Ernie said.

We cried together. When was the last time I cried with a friend? Ever?

"Strip Dance"

That night, the usual strip dance began as tape was taken off aching bodies to comments of, "ooooh, come see this!", "arrgh," and "that's disgusting."

Looking at one another's destroyed feet and choosing how to treat them became a group medical discussion, hovering between horror and laughter.

"Cut it," said Andy.

"Slice and drain," said Bez.

"Amputate," said Sharon.

I suffered more pain that day than ever in my life, including from all of the injuries I have sustained and the numerous surgeries I have undergone. But at the same time, in a primal sort of way, I felt more alive than ever before. I knew that today's and other Gobi moments would be etched in my mind forever and that I would soon look back on them with affection. Maybe it was a case of knowing that what didn't kill me would make me stronger.

A deep bond developed among all of us in our tent. John had been in first place from four hours into the race, faster than I by an hour or so, and I was leading Louie by 15 minutes. The time accordion stretched all the way to almost 10 hours just in our tent. But we all shared the same experiences, including running in a river, on rolling rocks in a canyon, on soft clay dunes, and up a nasty hill, as well as getting lost, befriending a fellow competitor while running, and being stuck eating dehydrated foods. If I recounted part of my day, someone else picked up on it and shared how it was for them. Although we competed against each other in the overall rankings, we found pleasure in supporting one another and respecting everyone's experiences and perceptions. We all suffered, but each in our own way.

I had slipped to tenth place overall and merrily went to the cyber-tent to blog. The emails were starting to come in.

email *Posted: 15-Jun-2009 12:04:34 PM*
Stéfan! Dude – you are so kicking ass! Got goose bumps reading your blog. Very inspiring – wishing I was there beside you (well ... not really – in spirit anyway). Enjoy the process. Don't keep asking yourself "when is this going to end" – instead – "man, this is going to end too soon - something I have trained for so hard and so long." Try and stay present and enjoy it – as much as you can. You are awesome! Keep it up, buddy. Phil

While I have received accolades before for good deeds, nothing compared with receiving support from back home during this ordeal. Everyone in the camp felt removed from civilization. I drew on these email comments for energy when needed.

We were down two marathons, four left to go.

CHAPTER 15

DAY THREE:
DIVINE INTERVENTION

Our greatest weakness lies in giving up.
The most certain way to succeed is always
to try just one more time.

—THOMAS EDISON, INVENTOR

June 16

Each day's race started at 9 a.m. That's what it said on our clocks, but the real time was closer to 6 a.m., meaning we got up each morning in total darkness. The Chinese government had determined that the Xinjiang autonomous region should be on Beijing time. So despite being four hours due west of the city by plane, that's the time we were on. It made for beautiful sunsets around 11 p.m.

Waking up to shredded feet, I hopped outside in the dark to ponder my options. I decided to tape plastic around the two worst toes. Thanks to Naproxen and Advil, they would be numb by start time.

We were alerted at briefing time to the three main parts of day three:

- *A start in wet farmlands*
- *A run up a dry riverbed*
- *Finish in a long steady mountain climb to 2,745 meters*

And we were told the conditions we could expect:

- *Moderate winds at 20 kilometers per hour*
- *Overcast and 35-degree temperature*

Slip Sliding Away

What was new to this day was running in a muddy, densely treed area that looked like a mini jungle for the first 15 kilometers. Slipping and sliding our way along, we were covered in wet dirt, head to toe. This was a desert? Many were cursing. Sticking to my psychological strategy, I laughed, imagining I was eight years old playing in the mud and thinking of what I looked like after many of my mountain biking rides in Toronto's Don Valley – either scene a picture perfect Tide commercial.

By then I had noticed that my vision was poor. At times I could see the course flags; at times not. Sometimes I could see their pink color; other times they looked white from a distance. I got lost twice in a densely treed area because I missed a flag. Managing my frustration whenever I lost time and was passed by other runners was a test, knowing how hard I would have to work to catch up.

The morning's highlight was a half-kilometer run down a wet river, running full speed in three to 15 centimeters of water. I could be a kid again; when was the last time I ran and splashed with abandon? How many times have I asked my kids not to step in puddles? I promised myself to soak my kids and start a splash fight.

Sabotage

Fast-forward two hours: We were now in a gorgeous dry riverbed. I was running alone. It happened again: for the third time that day I got lost. I ran upriver 500 meters looking for a location where logically there should have been a flag. There was none. I panicked, wondered about time lost, and, following "lost" protocol, retreated to the last flag I had seen.

From there I spotted a flag flapping at the top of a steep 30-meter high wall. It was fascinating; I was running in a crevasse now, after crawling up its face; it was a whole new world up there: an endless plateau of rolling hills. I started running to a flag every hundred meters. A mirage. There were no more flags.

Kevin Lepsoe, a Canadian banker at Morgan Stanley's Hong Kong office, had been sitting on the ground in a meditative state, trying to wait peacefully for others to arrive. I'd caught up to six runners, and another eight would catch up to me, including Louie. We were all running around trying to understand where to go. Now all of the runners from 8th position to 20th were up there.

People reacted in their own ways. Some were pissed off and were pouting; others actively searched for the next flag in an organized manner; still others argued and pointed the finger at the individuals they were following, saying they had felt they were taking the wrong direction. Some were resigned and looked to others for leadership. One common setback, and twelve different reactions, but all in one of two camps: screaming I'm a victim or looking for a solution.

I didn't handle it with grace. I was fuming. Where were the lessons from day one? I wondered.

As Kevin would say after the race: "Getting lost in day three was bittersweet. My first reaction was anger and to accuse one of the guys placed fourth to sixth in front of me. I figured the runners were in groups of three. The first three must have known where to go and so it must have been someone in the next group. I ran for about 20 minutes in a large semi-circle keeping an eye on where the last flag was. After not seeing any other flags, I came back to the one flag at the top of the ridge and just sat down and stretched.

"I knew people would eventually catch up, and in the worst case I could simply head down the hill and go backward. Just sitting there on the plateau was serene. It was beautiful. Having run throughout the race you don't really get a chance to enjoy the beauty of this part of the world. It was a bit of forced reaction and one of those slow-motion moments where you think, 'Wow, this place is so beautiful.' I got up after a few minutes and started rethinking my strategy to find the next flag and by then a few competitors had come up the hill."

Getting lost, especially after three hours on the course, is a terrible feeling. We decided to stick together and go back down into the river in order not to concede an advantage to anyone. If the climb up to the mesa was nasty, the slide down was even worse. While Kevin seemed to have been at peace, I was likely more put out than most. Or possibly we were simply cursed. Off balance, Kevin and I both fell and slid down 10 meters in the rocks, both of us getting badly banged up. Another 15 runners had now caught up; all that hard work wasted. I was now running next to people I hadn't seen during the previous three days. I snapped out of it and got going again.

Run, don't think! I told myself.

The flag foul-up had two benefits for the runners who had caught up: They were fresher than the rest of us, not having run off course, and they were getting an emotional lift from the experience of running with stronger runners. Some of them capitalized on their luck.

We later found the flags upriver; it was clear someone had deliberately moved them to send us in the wrong direction. Speculation was rampant about who had done it and why. All fingers pointed in one direction, but it was never confirmed.

Logistically, it was impossible to police the 500-plus small pink flags set up over 42 kilometers to orient racers on the mountainous desert.

Kevin said later: "I was pretty pissed that I had to bear the full brunt – 45 to 50 minutes – of someone's direct attempt to throw off the runners. Shortly after coming down from the plateau, I realized I couldn't run anymore. This was emotionally very tough. We were getting up to around 2,740 meters, the air was getting thin, and the air was getting cold. It was difficult to head up that last stretch, but I managed to stick with Shawn Harmon, who I felt helped carry me to the top, though he might have thought I helped him. The race is nothing without friendship."

Last Leg

After having pushed hard to make up some ground, all uphill in the riverbed, I arrived in bad shape at checkpoint 3. I was shaky and was losing my edge. For the first time in three days I became aware of what the volunteers were there to do. I felt humbled. In the absence of an appreciative gallery, such as your family and friends, or streets lined with cheering spectators, each checkpoint provided the just-in-time boost you so needed. Until then I had been completely transactional; now I talked to the volunteers. Why were they there? How could they be so generous as to labor alongside us? They had come all this way at their own expense, typically to support a friend, or spouse, but working for all of us in insufferable heat all day, and all to tap you on the back, give you your allotted water, and provide you with words of encouragement. Would I be able to give myself in this way for a week? Probably not.

The last leg was straight uphill, rising steadily for 250 meters, without a flat section, just relentlessly up. My pace was slower and I abandoned trying to make up for the time lost and let a few people get ahead of me. I was also unable to respond to being chased down. I heard my familiar self-defeating voice speaking the standard fare of "told you's" and "quitter."

I couldn't fight it. Instead, I started to amuse myself with it. I decided to name the voice. I settled on the name of someone

I know who is famous for passing negative judgments and considers everyone else an idiot. Just creating separation between me and "the voice" helped me move forward some more. The race was teaching me ways to expand my ability to handle the harsh criticisms and judgments I directed at myself, others, and my circumstances.

Thirty minutes later, I had been hoping for some kind of second wind to kick in after ingesting liquid sugar, but it never came. Unable to continue, I stopped and put a knee down. I was at a loss; there was nothing left in the tank. The first person to pass was Stephen Kodish, entered as part of Team LUNGevity but now running solo. Steve's father had stage 3 lung cancer and he was running to raise money for lung cancer and to lift his father's spirits and pay homage to him.

A Prayer, of Sorts

The best I could do was to ask for a divine intervention. I started calling for my own father for help, something I had never done before. Ironic, given that he likely had never run in his life except when teaching me how to ride a bike. I was hallucinating. I heard him answer, "Nice to hear from you on my birthday!" It was spooky enough to stand me up and get me to shuffle a few more steps.

My dad was a creative type. He didn't like sports and couldn't understand my passion for anything athletic as opposed to arts, music, or literature. We were close but we clashed on my life choices, from being in business to living in English Canada. He had turned out to be a good father and an extraordinary grandfather. Today he would be prouder knowing that I was on the board of an art gallery in Toronto than that I was running in the desert. I rejected many of the activities my dad pushed on me, growing up. He can rest in peace: love for the arts and writing did "go in." It just sat in a parking lot for 35 years or so first.

I got up and was now running 100 steps, and walking 100, but the tide was turning. Soon it was 75-25, 50-50, and then only walking, haggardly.

"Just one step at a time," I remembered coach Donna saying.

I collapsed again.

I got down on my knees again and started talking to my dad. June 16 would have been his 71st birthday. I started crying and asking for forgiveness.

"I'm sorry, Dad. I hope you're enjoying yourself up there and that there is a lot of red wine. I miss you."

I felt ashamed to have called up for help, on his birthday. It hit me that I should just love and cherish him. He had done his job, providing me with everything he could, and he and Mom had made the sacrifices all caring parents do to launch me into the world.

"I need help, Dad," I pleaded. "I don't have it in me to keep on going."

It broke his heart when he saw me head west to Ontario. He didn't like "les maudit anglais" and never understood why I left. It was the first time I had truly disappointed him. I was always sure that deep down he was proud to see me carving my own way.

Why was I thinking about my relationship with him on this day at this time? It seemed like despite being 45, stronger and fitter than he ever was, now that I was facing real adversity, I was going back to the well that encouraged me out of all the difficulties I had ever faced growing up. My parents had stood by me valiantly and lovingly as I found my path to adulthood.

He passed away so suddenly, never being able to fully see his grandkids. My dad was always present with me, but I realized in the desert that I wasn't engaging with him as much anymore. He loved architecture, travel, and was a practicing Catholic. My favorite way to be with him is to light up a candle when I see a church that captures my imagination, typically while traveling. We have pictures in the house to keep him in our lives and ensure that our kids never forget his generous, fun-loving way, his laughter and passion for life. We commissioned a painting of him holding a glass of red wine with a Tuscan backdrop for our wine cellar. He is smiling the way all wine lovers do, and he definitely passed his love of wines on to me.

The desert unearthed issues that had been deeply buried. Had I handled grieving and moving forward after his passing? My mom and I had fallen into a routine in which we didn't really talk about my dad. He left us suddenly, a heart attack while alpine skiing at his beloved Mont Saint-Sauveur, collapsing mid run, the horrific moment 25 meters in front of my mother. We rationalized that it was a great way for him to go, painlessly and while doing something he loved.

"It is the way we all should go," she said.

Deep inside, though, we harbored some pain: We felt robbed, with unresolved issues and without saying a proper goodbye. During the eulogy, I had made a pledge to seize the day going forward, with death being so random.

Now here I was in the desert, kneeling, revisiting that day.

"Dad, am I doing enough to stay connected to you? Have I drifted away? Am I being the best son I can be to my mother?"

Sobbing in the desert, I found the energy to manufacture a few disempowering answers to my questions. I decided to hold on to my discomfort and to engage my mother in the discussion upon returning.

Pain is temporary. Quitting is forever.
−LANCE ARMSTRONG, TOUR DE FRANCE CHAMPION

I slowly came to, realizing that I still had to finish the last leg of the day's race. I noticed that my private moment had been taking place right on the course's final ascent. A dozen runners had passed me. Many of them had taken a "run-on" role in my little drama. Some uttered some warm words – "You're almost to the finish" – while others tapped me on the back. Some were oblivious to my collapse, either because they were single-mindedly focused on finishing, were blocking the negative sight, had chosen to retain their energy to concentrate, or possibly were just confused about how to deal with a fallen comrade.

I stood up and started running.

Immediately I heard the bongo drums and let them pull me to the finish line. The ritual was the same every time. A drummer, upon catching a glimpse of a runner, started drumming, banging progressively faster the closer he or she got to the finish, with an all-out jam as the runner crossed. The simple ritual produced exquisite moments, transporting most of us to running at a pace beyond what we thought possible.

After five and a half hours, having been first lost on the plateau and then in my thoughts, I hobbled into Camp 4, suitably called Heaven's Gate, thanking my father.

Kevin, with whom I had fallen when we were descending the plateau, was in bad shape. I searched the camp to get him some help from Sharon, the most popular person in our tent because she was so devoted to everyone's welfare and was a physiotherapist by trade.

I was furious at what had happened on the plateau, how we had fallen down in trying to get back to the course, because of someone's trickery. Kevin was philosophical about the situation, which shocked me.

He admitted that framing happiness in the right context was very difficult for A-type personalities like him. He said he does so by balancing his ambitious nature with "the constant appreciation for what I have."

That night, instead of lamenting what could have been a top ten finish overall, possibly top five, and instead facing the prospect of a ruined second Gobi attempt, this time because someone had moved the flags, he focused on rebuilding his shoe for greater ankle support. He folded and molded tape into an inner arch support to ease the pain and help him continue the race.

One thing is for sure: When adversity hits, you become intimately aware of the possibilities within you. A competitor told me it must have seemed counterintuitive to me to help the one Canadian who stood ahead of me.

"Not at all," I responded.

In a race this long, most people developed great admiration for everyone there, especially someone like Kevin who was returning for a second time. Almost anyone would drop what they were doing to help you out. It would be a perfect blueprint for an organization.

Another interesting story was how two solo entrants, Diana Hogan-Murphy and David Pearse, were working together. Diana's competitive spirit soared to new heights after the first day when she took the lead among women, and Dave adjusted to new role: helping her win by pushing and testing himself to a new level.

Dave had approached the race seriously but his main objective remained "being in a beautiful remote place, with kindred people, living in a subsistence lifestyle."

It all changed after the first day. Dave shared that while there were numerous heated exchanges between him and Diana, they leveraged their complementary traits: Diana's charging style, his ability to finish strong. What seemed to me to be a great sacrifice on his part to choose to suffer for a week to help a friend win was, in fact, exactly the opposite.

"It was a real privilege," said Dave. "I witnessed a champion's courage and determination from close in."

There is much to be learned in a win-win partnership. They strategized each day about the course and their plan and worked together to resolve problems. Diana eventually won the event. Dave had pushed Diana very hard on the last stretch of the long 84-kilometer day, and she sustained injuries to each of her feet. The two were hard at work on the rest day to mend them.

Now, at 2,740 meters of altitude in our horseshoe-shaped bivouac, the night was cold and breezy, only four degrees Celsius. Time for the fleece hat, I decided.

I hung around the fire with Todd Handcock and Peter Symonds, two Canadians living in Hong Kong who traveled to the Gobi together.

"I ask myself why, why, why am I here?" said Todd, then a vice president at British Telecom. "I guess because the opportunity was there to do something physically and mentally harder than I had ever done before. It was a chance to push myself outside of my comfort zone and experience something that was out on the edge. It was something that I could reflect back on and say that 'I did it' rather than 'I should have done it' – carpe diem."

Peter took a softer view. "It was a way of challenging myself, testing myself to some degree and therefore bringing greater meaning and substance to life."

Many people got sick that night. Despite our differences in age, values, styles, countries, and preparation, my tentmates were my companions, my safe harbor. We were a unit caring for each other. Each day was complete only once everyone had made a safe return. Things would not be the same with Ernie's planned departure from camp.

While recovering from a day's run, I walked back on the course and positioned myself where I could see the heroism of each participant. Nothing gave me more joy than seeing Bez or Sharon round the corner.

Said Bez, almost every day: "I got that wonderful euphoric

feeling crossing the finishing line knowing that I'd completed the task at hand and given it my all."

I got as much energy from her elation as I did from mine. Giving her and Sharon the welcome hug always made me teary.

Sharon would later recount: "Having completed the Gobi gives me a feeling of great satisfaction and accomplishment. It helps me in my life now. I know that I am physically, mentally, and emotionally strong enough to cope in adverse situations with difficult people, children, etc. When I have moments of self-doubt, I subconsciously, or even consciously, know that I can do it because I've raced across the Gobi."

I remembered these words from Norman Vincent Peale that night, which I held onto in any economic recession: "Tough times don't last, tough people do."

I would "grow" the size of my thighs and heart feeding on the inbound emails from family, friends, or complete strangers before going to bed. Sometimes these communications had me crying; other times laughing.

emails Posted: 17-Jun-2009 02:12:39 PM
Your feet are numb and so am I. I'm trying hard not to worry and focus on the pain endured ... Your girls are with you and love you ... Just come home not completely mutilated!! xoxo
Leslie

Posted: 17-Jun-2009 05:22:56 AM
I think a sponsorship from Band-Aid is in order if you do this again. You're doing amazingly well for being a rookie at this! Keep it up. Me? I'm just doing emails.
Doug Poad

Posted: 16-Jun-2009 07:39:29 AM
great blog mate, not so good about people laying false trails ... not in the spirit of the gobi. keep on! My wife is one of those coming in at 9:28 today number 86 liz luya.
ross eathorne

CHAPTER 16

DAY FOUR:
HEAVEN'S GATE

*Life is not measured by the
number of breaths we take, but by the
moments that take our breath away.*

–UNKNOWN

June 17

The briefing was simple on day four:

- *300-meter climb to Heaven's Gate and descent*
- *Canyon run-out*

I'd been briefed by Mehmet to sprint out to the base of Heaven's Gate, about two kilometers away. It was a gentle climb uphill but at high altitude. I could deal with my exploding heart once there.

I did as he advised, and the prize was a good location in the single-file climbing queue. Because of the boulders, eight ladders at different heights awaited for us to negotiate the steep narrow sections to a new upper shelf. The pace slowed because only one racer could be on a ladder at a time. We climbed about 45 meters of altitude this way: sprinting on the rocks between each ladder and climbing them as quickly and safely as possible.

Then the space opened up. The ascension here was so steep that I got down on all fours and clawed my way up for another 180 meters; we passed each other, all the way to the 10,000 foot summit, like turtles racing.

What goes up must come down, I thought. My lungs were pounding in my chest and I wished I had done more hill repeats and stair climbing in my training. At that altitude, the barometric pressure is 30 percent lower than at sea level, meaning you intake 30 percent less oxygen per breath than at sea level. Even though we had climbed to the altitude gradually, over a few days, racing up for 300 meters put me in such a state of hyperventilation that I couldn't settle down until much later. My lungs required great draughts of air, yet I felt I was breathing through a straw.

With my lungs unable to produce enough oxygen, and the thighs my mother bequeathed to me defaulting, I stopped at the top, in tears of pain. This was the signature view of the race, standing at the foot of the highest natural arch in the world.

Shipton's Arch

The arch was first reported in the west by British mountaineer Eric Shipton, in his 1947 book *Mountains of Tartary*. Shipton's Arch is 365 meters tall and about 55 meters across. Interestingly, Guinness World Records had it as the highest arch in the world but the listing was dropped when editors could not the 1947 reference after visiting the area and being unable to find it. The arch was relocated by arch-hunting westerners and reported in the May 2000 issue of National Geographic in an article *"Journey to Shipton's Lost Arch."*

I felt a close connection with my dad when at the top of a rise, I stood under Heaven's Gate.

I thought about him, stopped for a picture, looked around, took a deep breath, and ran down. Thirty seconds had to suffice for my view of what was to natural rock formations what the pyramids are to tombs.

Tentmate David Breakwell captured these moments later when he told me, "On every adventure, you are guaranteed that you will indeed catch your breath, not just through your physical labors, that's a given, but at the sheer magnificence of your surroundings. It isn't just when you cross that finishing line that the sheer euphoria, the tsunami of emotion will wash over you. It can creep up on you at the most unexpected of times and it simply overpowers you. You think of home, your wife, and your children. At that moment in time, the most precious and beautiful things seem magnified ten thousand fold."

With an appreciative chuckle, he continued: "You feel them with you and draw your strength from them. To me, those moments are the best; they find out your deepest emotions and lay them bare. It's cathartic. The race demands your all; you have to give everything you have to triumph, and that triumph is so sweet. These events are not so much life changing as life enhancing. I don't come back a different person from these events; they help to make me the person I am."

We went down in parallel while others were still climbing. It was the first time runners were together at the same location while in the middle of the race. It was a two-way revelation. Those of us in the front marveled at the tenacity of the back of the pack, while they marveled at the speed of the front. It highlighted one of the communal cornerstones of desert racing.

Norma Bastidas said it best: "These events are the only sports in the world where elite and novice interact and race as equals. It is common to see elite athletes stay and cheer the slower runners and discuss the day's events at night with anyone of any rank or order. This type of camaraderie is non-existent in other sports."

My high recklessness quotient kicked into high gear, and I went down fast. I felt as if I was part of my own climb-chase scene in the 007 movie *Casino Royale*, jumping from rock to rock. The climb had been so painful that it took me 90 minutes to cover 8.5 kilometers and get back down to checkpoint 1.

This part of the race had been the most demanding for my right knee. Was it the painkillers? I don't know, but it held just fine. Dr. Cameron would be proud. I had been wondering from the moment I had signed up if the knee would hold and now felt free to push harder given that the worst section of the entire race was behind me.

Canadian Todd Handcock had the same experience with his reconstructed left ACL. "The last time I thought about my knee was prior to the race. The next time I thought about it was after I had finished. Whether I mentally blocked out the pain or not, it just held up in a way that I did not expect."

We then raced on donkey trails, climbing and descending a furious range of 300-foot-tall canyons for an hour. Each climb killed my quads as I sprint-walked on the vertical face; each descent required a quick risk assessment: dare to run or play it safe? A run could put my knee at risk or induce a fall in the rocks; walking and sliding was the safer approach but slow. I was comfortable descending; it was akin to picking a line for skiing or down-hilling on my mountain bike. I had lost ground ascending, chased uphill by a competitor who used poles to pace and push himself, but put distance between us on the descents where I attacked.

Ultimately we were spat out onto the dry riverbed where I hooked up with young Chris Davies, a 22-year-old professional British seaman. He was doing well in the race despite not wearing any gear of his own – he was the poor soul who had lost his backpack on the airport connection in Beijing. Many of the competitors had pitched in gear and food for him.

He told me that once he arrived in Kashi and realized his bag had not made it, he worried but never panicked. He was more concerned that he had come all this way, trained full time for two months, spent a ton, and wasn't going to be allowed to compete. All he wanted was the opportunity to push himself – and he did so in a way many of us wouldn't have dared.

"This race became something I *had* to do," he said. "I was not concerned that I didn't have the things I'd trained with or planned to have. What I love about this sport is its simplicity: shoes, shorts preferably, and that's about it. It's a sport you can muddle through really with a good, strong will."

He said the only thing he should have been a little more worried about was a sleeping bag.

"Those first two nights were very, very cold. I thought it best not to complain or let anyone know. I knew there would be people with far worse problems soon enough, and I was hoping not to become one of them, putting my energy into that."

At the time, I was so concerned about the race itself I was oblivious to his issues. My self-absorption had blinded me to a special situation.

It was ironic to be running with a seaman in the desert. His yacht job took him around the world, garnering him an international group of friends and clients. He decided to help one of them, Médecins Sans Frontières, and decided on the Gobi race as the way to do it. In school he had been a cross-country runner and after school he had run multi-stage races, including the Great Russian Race.

"Back then I told myself, 'one day, a desert,'" he said.

Chris and I worked very hard and collaborated for 30 kilometers, running together for four hours, side by side at first, quickly choosing to draft each other for speed to put time on the field. We were moving very fast and both felt strong. One of us focused on orienteering and setting the pace, and the other on providing encouragement from behind while reporting progress on the field at the rear. We discussed our protocols; we decided we would help each other until the last kilometer and then it would be each man for himself.

If you start to feel good during an ultra,
don't worry, you will get over it.

−GENE THIBEAULT, RUNNER

I cracked with 15 kilometers to go, but Chris stuck to our agreement and paced me despite my struggling. Before long, I could barely move and we were alternating runs and walks as had happened to me on day three. I asked him to leave me behind because I couldn't find the energy to continue; I was barely just walking. It had been six hours of running by then, and I had never run this long before. I waited for my second wind, but it failed to show.

My daily food program had worked well but wasn't designed for more than six hours. As my daily ration was insufficient, I started opening my day five pack to ingest as much gel and electrolytes as I could find, disregarding my planned rationing and incurring time fussing with my gear, opening zippers to search for food buried into my pack.

All this allowed Ron Hertshen from Israel to close the gap. Not only were Chris and I struggling and growing frustrated, we also got lost and missed a turn. We looked back and saw Ron one kilometer behind us waving us back. He had hunted us down for four hours, now he was our prey.

The sugar finally metabolized 15 minutes later and gave me a surge of energy. It was my turn to pay Chris back for his support. I took the lead position, leaning into the surging 30-kilometer-an-hour headwind all the way in, while Chris drifted. The roles had reversed; he had now reached his limit. I had offered to let him leave me behind, and now he was doing the same. As agreed, with one kilometer to go, we split up and with my adrenaline pumping, I bolted. I wanted to honor our agreement and also let him know I was strong as he was just behind me in the overall standings in 11th place. Five minutes later, I looked over my shoulder and he was out of sight as we ran along a ridge with blind spots.

With the aid of glucose, the finish was as magical as the seven hours of running bonded with a fellow competitor. Luckily, a moment of soberness hit me. What was I doing racing in alone? I stopped dead in my tracks five meters short of the finish and waited for Chris. A couple of minutes later, he arrived, shaking his head in wonderment that I was there. We ran to the finish hand in hand, a perfect ending after so much teamwork. It was my best moment of the whole week. I was teary-eyed to have conquered Heaven's Gate.

Kevin Lepsoe rolled into camp 12 hours later after the day started, because of his injury with me on the plateau the previous day. Not only had we all climbed to Shipton's Arch together, Kevin had spent his day at the back of the field after having spent the first three days at the front.

"You really feel like shit at times," he said, "but when you look at some of the other competitors, especially the less fit ones, the ones constantly in the medical tent or the ones stumbling into camp late at night, you realize how lucky you are, how much stronger they are than you."

One day prior, he was the first Canadian. Now I was.

That night, filled with the memories of a beautiful natural arch and having completed my longest run ever, I went to bed shivering in the 50-kilometer-an-hour wind and rapidly descending temperatures. I also started thinking about more collaborative agreements with my business competitors. Running with Chris showed me that thriving in a tough economy may call for cooperative agreements with my competition. Even competitors like Chris, who were half my age.

Emails kept pouring in, dozens at a time, sometimes to offer comfort on what lay ahead, or just to share that they were along with me on the journey. There I was in one of the loneliest places on earth, feeling something indescribable but kind of like a digital hug. I experienced firsthand the power of encouragement, the way a child does. It gave me the momentum to do the same and adopt the role of cheerleader in the tent to comfort others.

I started to scan for reasons to give a hug or hold someone who had been beaten up by the long day. At the same time, I was also confronted by my business-like attitude at work and even at home where it seems people needed to earn my accolades and support. In many ways I had been hardening as a CEO, receiving little empathy and forgetting how to offer it. With the various leadership roles I had, I made a note that I needed to reconnect with my grateful side, which had somehow gone dormant during the recession.

> **emails** Posted: 17-Jun-2009 09:48:55 AM
> We're dazzled by your +++ approach and achievement, Stefan.
> Strength for tomorrow! Jim Warrington + team
>
> Posted: 17-Jun-2009 10:38:02 AM
> Stéf – Your story is unbelievable. My feet hurt just reading. I know
> tomorrow is the bad day and when all hell breaks loose in your brain
> - which it undoubtedly will - I hope you think of how proud your family
> must be of you. Your daughters have a hell of a story to be telling their
> classmates - and it will be even more amazing after you do
> 85 tomorrow. Good luck. We are all cheering you on and telling
> your story with great pride.
> Doug Keeley

CHAPTER 17

DAY FIVE:
CAT AND MOUSE

*I had as many doubts as anyone else.
Standing on the starting line,
we're all cowards.*

−ALBERTO SALAZAR, THREE-TIME WINNER OF THE NYC MARATHON

June 18

I hadn't really slept thus far. That night I decided to take all my sleeping pills at once to knock myself out before the big day. It worked. Strong winds hit us in the middle of the night, blowing the tent off. Everyone was hard at work outside fixing it. At least that's what they told me in the morning. I slept through it all, really endearing myself to my tentmates.

85 Kilometers

The start of this long day – the 85-kilometer run – was actually an hour away from the camp. We hopped on a bus to get there at 5 a.m., which completely threw our morning routines out of whack.

The bus drive gave me too much time to think about the distance that lay ahead. Was it possible to run this long? I wondered. We were unceremoniously dumped at the start site and everyone scrambled to tape their feet in the cold morning breeze. Picture more than a hundred people shivering and furiously taping their feet on 15 minutes' notice before the most epic run of their lives. Hardly the kind of set up I expected. Without coffee and time or final jitters, I was cranky and slow to get going and got only one foot taped up. I chose to take the start with everyone as opposed to starting later, fully taped and alone.

That morning on the bus, I finally clued in that I was in a position to win top Canadian and top in the 40 to 49 range. I had gone at it hard in the first four days, racing young and old.

I changed my thinking and tactics at this point in the race. I would start slowly, not all-out to gauge what I was capable of that day. I shifted my mindset to running defensively. I knew the trade-off was sliding one or two positions in the overall standings; it would be worth it if I could remain healthy, focus on not getting injured, and be watchful to lock in my position where I was the leader.

Playing defense was definitely not my modus operandi. I have always preferred to go hard and try to hold on as opposed to pacing myself. Even in some of my favorite activities, such as golf, I struggle to match play and hold the lead. Implosion is always around the corner. I was hoping to get a breakthrough today.

My strategy for surviving the day was to drug myself. I would ingest an extra strength 400 mg Advil every hour in addition to the daily Naproxen and 800 mg of electrolyte pills. I wasn't thinking clearly. The 4,000 mg of Advil would end up destroying my kidneys, but I rarely felt my legs.

The long day (as it is called) started. I bolted out to show that I was not going to go down without a fight, meaning I had folded on my defense-first strategy. The beginning of the race was a long, arduous, visually unrewarding climb uphill. Everyone from #9 to #20 was in a pack and I stayed as close to the front as I could. There was then a difficult uphill and a joyful, steep downhill. The latter served me well; while many tiptoed or slid down, I went with abandon, landing flat footed with my body tilted forward, picking downhill lines. Ludvig, two positions behind me overall, and I ran so fast we high fived each other at the bottom, thrilled.

I finally came to my senses. It occurred to me I should be careful going forward and not risk injury now that I had made it so far into the race.

Who Will Break?

Soon, déjà vu: We were in a large dry riverbed with loose stones requiring the utmost vigilance. We had the Tian Shans at our back and it felt like we were on the home stretch now, for the next 65 kilometers. It was relatively flat here, and everyone caught up, forming a loose pack. Talking was kept to a minimum to conserve energy. I checked that everyone was there, marked them, and we ran together, including Ron, Ludvig, and Chris, competing for overall standings. In the pack also were Blain Davis, a personal trainer from Edmonton, and my friend Louie, vying for first Canadian and first in the 40-50 age category.

Running 85 kilometers would be a new experience for all of us except Blain, who had previous experience running deserts. Knowing I was about to spend a lot of time with myself, I made a pact that this was a good day to become my own best friend, a tall order for someone so self-critical.

Every 15 minutes, one of the individuals in the pack attacked and I felt I had to respond every time because we were all close in the overall standings, although most of them were just behind me.

Who is going to break? I thought it would be me. In time, the younger guys stepped up their attacks and I chose to defend my position, accepting a move back in the overall standings.

The guys competing in my age group were all slowly fading

away, including Louie, whose haggard running suggested he would have a bad day. Barring an unforeseen event, I had bagged the age group sub-category race. I turned my focus to the Canadian part of the battle.

Two hours later, only Blain, who was second, remained. We would stay together for nine hours. While I had ended up in the Gobi to challenge myself out of a wayward mindset, Blain had a much higher purpose.

"My son, who is now six years old, has cystic fibrosis," he told me. "I had struggled to figure out how I could help. I wanted to pick something that I wasn't good at to raise money for my son's fatal disease. I'm fit but was not a runner until I signed up for the Marathon des Sables and converted myself into one. In a weird way, I needed to suffer and still do because I know that my son will soon suffer infinitely more in his life."

My tears evaporated immediately in the 40-degree heat.

Every once in a while Blain pushed and watched for my response. Grunting, I responded and matched him as we played our game of cat and mouse in the desert.

Never look back unless you are planning to go that way.
—HENRY DAVID THOREAU, AUTHOR

Finally, after seven hours of being very aware of my surroundings, constantly looking over my shoulder to assess where all the marked competitors were, I became annoyed with the game and decided to stop running defensively.

My Own Path

It occurred to me that I had been looking behind and sideways a little too much in life, putting too much emphasis on comparing positions as opposed to carving my own path free from comparisons. Appraising higher standards had fueled my drive to excel, but excelling came with many traps: There was always someone richer, better, smarter, faster, thinner, or stronger. It's not that I was envious, but that I was failing to celebrate my own life for what it was. I knew I suffered from always thinking that I could do better. That was fine for me, but what was it doing to my kids? Was I comparing them with others instead of honoring them in their own uniqueness? I concluded it was time to find a better balance between who I was and who I could be.

Something I had heard came back to me: "Love the kids you have, not the ones you want."

Heavy stuff when you're just trying to put one foot in front of the other in a dusty 49 degrees Celsius, but somehow I was slowly taming an inner voice that had been hyperactive for 40 years.

Pushing each other had its rewards: We caught up to Ludvig and passed him, but were passed by Mitchell and Ari Stocks, an experienced father-and-son duo who had been part of the team that had imploded earlier in the week. Now they could run their own race, having dropped their third man who could not keep up.

My tactic of not looking back didn't translate into a material change: Blain was hanging around.

For the first time, for extended periods of time, the sand was beach-like soft, requiring a change in foot planting to glide over it.

"It's the same as in the Sahara," said Blain.

He went on to share the lead-up to his first desert.

"July 20th, 2007, we had driven down to my parents to help them move. Early Saturday on the 21st, we received a call from our neighbor across the street. 'Your house is on fire ... the whole block is on fire ...'" An arsonist had set fire to a three-story condominium under construction behind our house. It was quickly engulfed in flames and the wind blew flames to the row of homes adjacent. Our home and 17 other homes were burned to the ground. We arrived back just in time to see it fall. So after the shock of losing literally everything we owned, we picked ourselves up to realize that we had our family intact. No one was injured. We had the love and support of family and friends to walk alongside us. We prevailed. Of course, I lost all my race gear, passport, and all, in the fire. I had to improvise to get myself to Egypt."

As had happened before, the desert's haziness started playing havoc with my eyes as I tired. Slowly but surely, I started running hesitantly, never knowing for sure where the next flag was. Having Blain with me turned out to be a blessing; his vision was laser like. Soon enough, his eyes became mine. Even though I would have liked to have won the day as top Canadian, trying to go without him meant I might have got lost, giving him the opportunity to outrun me anyway; he was fit the way only a personal trainer is fit.

After almost nine hours by his side, it had become apparent that no one was going to be dominant that day. We agreed to finish together as top Canadians for the day. I thought I had enough of a lead overall that it would be almost impossible to be caught up on the final day, which was a mere 10 kilometers long. Mission accomplished.

We were fatigued and our pace was slowing without the need to push each other anymore. Now ten hours into it, we were settling into a drawn-out meditative jog to the finish. I felt I was also running for his son at that moment.

Sleep running, we heard footsteps and saw Kevin fly by at full speed. He must have had a miraculous recovery, coming out of nowhere like that. Among Canadians, he had built up a lead on the first three days but had given all of it back on day four.

We were shocked; we thought he was behind for good. It took me a couple of minutes to collect myself. Running the math in my head, I wondered if I was enough ahead of him to win top Canadian – and if I could respond even if I wanted to. We were about 15 kilometers away from the finish. For an instant I let myself drift and just accepted that I had messed up. I started cursing the defensive strategy. Kevin was disappearing into the haze, about 300 meters ahead.

"We can kiss the idea of being today's first Canadians goodbye," I told Blain.

I recalled the vision I had painted for myself of looking back on the long day and feeling proud that I had given everything I had to compete.

"Chase Kevin down with me," I said. "Just for sport." He declined.

Life is often compared to a marathon, but I think it is more like being a sprinter; long stretches of hard work punctuated by brief moments in which we are given the opportunity to perform at our best.
−MICHAEL JOHNSON, OLYMPIC 400M CHAMPION

A Good Hour

The next hour I will cherish forever. After having run 235 kilometers in five days and 70 already that day, I ran the fastest 15 of my life, chasing Kevin as if he had taken something from me. I'd come this far, might as well get to full exhaustion and collapse and have no regrets. Kevin knew exactly what was going on; he frequently looked over his shoulder to assess my progress. He is an elite runner and for the first time I felt I was too. With 8 kilometers to go, still in pursuit of Kevin, I sprinted by Chris Davies, who cheered me on with a high five as I sped by.

The pain was acute but the joy of pushing myself beyond the limits I thought I had gave me wings. I was teary, but pushing all the way in. It was as if I was running for my life. When was the last time I had pushed this hard for anything?

Ask yourself: Can I give more?
The answer is usually: Yes.
−PAUL TERGAT, MARATHON RECORD HOLDER

I never caught Kevin. As it turns out, Kevin was actually more than three hours behind overall but the moment he passed me turned out to be a key impetus for me. I ran all the way to collapse and crossed the finish line with a three-minute delay, about the same as when I decided to pursue him. He saw me coming and cheered me in. We hugged, laughed, and I was filled up knowing I had given it my all.

To quote Mehmet who observed, from running the Gobi, "In life, you must be grateful and honor your competitors for having them show you what you have."

Kevin helped me see what was possible within me.

I thought about times at work when a colleague gets the promotion we thought we deserved, or when a client awards business to a competitor, or at home when we fail to be true to our commitments and connectedness slips away from us. Today's run showed me I need to alter my course upward, even with the help of a competitor, as opposed to dwelling in loss and spiraling down further.

> *If I am still standing at the end of the race,*
> *hit me with a board and knock me down,*
> *because that means I didn't run hard enough.*
> —STEVE JONES, MARATHON RECORD HOLDER

Here's how Kevin recounts that day.

"The long 80-kilometer day I was walking with difficulty and was in around 90th by the 20-kilometer mark. I remembered how depressed I was in the 2008 Gobi race, walking like Frankenstein for 18 hours.

"Around the 30-kilometer mark, something triggered in my brain and I just started to run through the pain. I somehow got lifted out of it and felt like I was floating the rest of the race. I finished the last 35 to 40 kilometers in just over four hours, much faster than any of my other days, which to me was one of my greatest running accomplishments ever.

"I remember vividly the moment I caught up to you and

Blain around the 65 mark or so. I had passed a number of competitors leading up to them. Most of the ones I passed were moving slowly; they were exhausted. I knew as I passed that you wouldn't let me go so easily."

I feel blessed to have had a handful of moments that I believe were "out of body" experiences: the kind in which you watch yourself from a distance. This happens when everything is clicking, a rare fleeting moment. I have had it snowboarding in powder, chasing friends in the trees at high speed, or windsurfing in big waves when I was one with the environment, or the time when I had my career round, playing golf. It is beautiful when it happens, and so precious. I had that for a full 75 minutes on this day of the race. I had thought I was done and yet somehow there was still gas in the tank.

email Posted: 23-Jul-2009 05:49:34 AM
well done Stefan. a great inspiration to us all. some people talk
about doing ... others simply do it. you will cherish each and every
blister, bug bite and scar forever.
howard breen

CHAPTER 18

DAY SIX: REST

*I*t ain't over till the fat lady sings.

–*UNKNOWN*

June 19

Coming after the 85-kilometer long stage, day six is designed to allow everyone to catch up. Many runners will spend the night running. Some will stop and lie down in an organized shelter at kilometer 50. Others will pull out their sleeping bags and lay them down in the desert to catch a few winks. Huzefa Mehta, an Indian living in California, is no stranger to these types of races, having run the Marathon des Sables and Jordan Cup and climbed Mount McKinley, a vicious mountain. Huzefa told the story of how he was walking around at 1 a.m. and stumbled on three others, who were sleeping in the middle of the desert. He decided to put his sleeping bag next to theirs. I laughed so hard at his description of how his unsuspecting bedmates reacted when they woke up next to a stranger.

That morning, still on a high from the previous day, I decided to compare my experience of the last few days with that of my life. Where did my experience fit in terms of what brought me joy in life? When was I at my best, realizing my potential? When was I joyful and great to be around? When was I growing as an individual? When was I making a contribution? When was I happiest?

The picture came into view rapidly. For quite some time now I have maintained a list of my top 20 life moments. Half of them revolve around traveling or some sort of adventure. Half of the others are the big family events – wedding, engagement, and births – and the balance are personal achievements. The Gobi was going to make its way onto my top 20, six years after the birth of my youngest daughter, Jade, made it on the board. Aging is not your friend when you do this exercise because it forces you to drop parts of your own history to make room for new experiences, and it brings into focus where you're focusing your attention chronologically – on the past, present, or future.

I finished writing and saw some competitors rolling in. My new friend Rob Follows came in with his wife Katrina, some twenty-seven hours after the start. My heart went out to them. I doubt I would have the stamina to be on my feet for that long, but this was second nature for them, because they were climbers first.

Unplugged

I was starting to relax and, after posting a message about the previous day's incredible finish, I compared notes with Todd Handcock, discussing what our respective families might be doing right now. He went on a tangent.

"This run is the first time in my adult life that I have been truly unplugged for an entire week. No laptop, no BlackBerry, no mobile phone, no TV, no radio, no newspaper. Other than the ability to blog from the cyber tent, I've been unplugged from the rest of the world. When do any of us ever turn off like that anymore?"

For me the answer was never, until now.

De-wiring was truly mind clearing and re-energizing.

Who would have thought that I'd be refreshed by the desert! I found that my brain shifted to a state of complete clarity and fogginess at the same time. You look around and there is not another soul to be seen you are in the middle of the desert, close to nowhere, and you just sink into a repetitive relaxed pace, your awareness focusing on every step because of the challenge of the terrain. At the same time, the difficulty of each step becomes second nature and requires no thought at all because you become so in tune with the environment."

I had to own up to the fact that I was good at "doing" but "being" was difficult for me. While it came easy to some, for me it required a conscious effort. Being connected to the office is the prime culprit for me. I knew the kids as they got older would soon be asking me to unhook from the BlackBerry the same way I would ask them to get off Facebook in the years to come. I don't recall ever being disconnected from the office unless it was for a few minutes while doing an activity that required total concentration.

As for not being in the moment, here's a case in point. Around midday, the rest day was getting to me. My decision to take off my tape and bathe in the stream caused my body to let down its defenses. I was punished for my error, big time. I had to visit the medic for antibiotics when infections flared up. Which led me to a grousing and boring evening in my tent.

Your playing small does not serve the world.
There's nothing enlightened about shrinking so that
other people won't feel insecure around you.
–MARIANNE WILLIAMSON, AUTHOR

Despite having outstanding tentmates, I decided that the lack of privacy had now gotten to me. Just like that, so close to the finish line, and for no reason that I could pinpoint, I had become my own self-appointed saboteur and was no longer having fun. Why had I signed up for this? I asked myself.

That night, the RacingThePlanet organization was celebrating its 20th race by launching fireworks, a seminal event for the organization. Most were there to witness and be part of it. I celebrated by putting on my earplugs. I think my spirit infected a few of my tentmates, too, who also missed the symbolic event.

I wrote about it honestly in the blog I sent that day, completely depressed. The media like failures; it makes for good reading. The rest day would end up getting more media pickup than any of the others.

email Posted: 25-Jun-2009 04:21:37 PM
Stefan, I just read your blog from start to finish. Wow! Like everyone else, I'm astounded and in awe. And that's just at your writing skills. You've got another career ahead of you. I very much enjoyed your description of losing your mental focus and your body's unfortunate response. And yet – football-sized, puss-oozing feet be damned – you finished the race. Bravo!
Patrick Allossery

CHAPTER 19

DAY SEVEN: THE FINAL PUSH

The miracle isn't that I finished. The miracle is that I had the courage to start.

–JOHN BINGHAM, AUTHOR

June 20

We were bused in from the desert to have that last, seventh-day glory run in the old city of Kashi. The course started 1 kilometer outside the core and led to the entry of the old fortressed city. It was a memorable day for all competitors, with an undertone of sadness at the same time. It was the end of an epic adventure, for one thing, and would be run in an old part of town made of raw earth and about to be destroyed.

I asked Louie if he wanted to run together and he agreed. Shortly after the start, he was gone and I couldn't catch up with my newfound wobbly feet. It really is difficult to move at someone else's pace.

The carry-over from the rest day was with me. I ran the longest and slowest 10 kilometer run ever, good enough for second last Canadian out of 13, and roughly 20 minutes off my fast training times.

The fast times were below 50 minutes, although the top runners routinely can go 20 percent faster when not carrying a backpack or having recently run 240 kilometers.

When you have the wrong mindset, small challenges become amplified. I got lost. I was overwhelmed by the stench of the exposed garbage. The thousand-year-old cobbles poked my feet, small hills looked like mountains to walk, and I was annoyed by the children who ran with me. I had wanted to witness Kashi's old city before it was obliterated to become an oversized Beijing-constructed Mao square. However, trapped in a victim mindset, I couldn't get myself to be in the moment.

Grunting my way came Nicola Fontanesi, an Italian banker whom I hadn't met before. He encouraged me along, twice pulling me as we crossed the line hand in hand. It was emotional for many, but not for me. I later saw the pictures of each finisher, most of them looking like they had just won the lottery. Mine looked like I was attending a funeral.

Back to Reality

Shortly after crossing the line, with medal around my neck, a more primal need surfaced and I quickly overtook the pizza stand, stampeding over Ernie who was waiting for us to arrive. I found out quickly the effects of gluttony, getting sick by gorging on too much "human food."

We took the requisite pictures, promised each other to keep in touch, and within 30 minutes all I wished for was a bath. I let Louie take the room and started walking the streets of Kashi to locate a pair of oversized sandals in a city where I towered over everyone. I knew my feet would never fit my shoes again once let out. The local kids were puzzled by my bandaged feet.

An hour later, filthy, dusty, tired, and still carrying my backpack, I arrived at the hotel, sandals in hand. I ran an ice cold bath, put my fleece hat on, and slipped into the water. I stopped shivering within a few moments and shrank a couple of sizes over 90 minutes.

I tried to make sense of what had just happened and why I felt the way I did. I couldn't come up with any answers and just accepted it as the way it was. There was no need to block the feelings. Let them pass through, I thought. I slowly put myself back in the moment to enjoy the festivities that were to follow. The sacrifices I had made and the pain I had experienced was afforded to very few. So was completing the race. It was time to honor myself and just be happy.

After eight days of disconnection from my family, but for their emails of support, I phoned and woke up my mom, reassuring her that I was safe. I then spoke to Leslie and the kids; there was so much to say, yet I didn't know where to start. The conversation was short.

On that last day, I had slipped one spot, ceding to Ron Hertshten from Israel. Of all people, he was the perfect candidate because his family had flown in from Tel Aviv to cheer him on and had decided to put a target on my back. The day before, while both of us were blogging, he received an email from his ambitious mother who had issued him a challenge: pass the Canadian who was one minute ahead of him. The scene in the cyber-tent was comical. We were sitting next to each other but hadn't met yet. He turned over to the table and caught my attention.

"Do you know who Stéfan Danis is?" he asked.

I introduced myself and he then issued the family challenge. By then, I had already thrown in the towel.

Take it, I said. Then, remembering what my friend Jim Wood would always say when leaving a bar scene that was not hopping to his liking: you can stick a fork in me – I'm done!

Ron beat me by 20 minutes, like a real champ.

Later that night I was able to thank my lucky star for

what I had just experienced. At 45, even though I still clearly needed to work on finishing stronger, when was I likely again to be the main actor in a story where I exceeded my own expectations?

There was a recurring theme for me to think about: Why did I rob myself of a special moment? Worse, did I rob others, too? On my last night, in a hotel in Kashi, I came up with a list of clean-ups. I would later have the joy of sincerely acknowledging the people in my life; I even took to doing it daily to negate my general tendency to notice what didn't work as opposed to what did.

When had I last been left to deal with true physical and mental adversity on my own? Not sure. I will cherish the Gobi as a moment in my life when I felt alive as rarely before while at the same time being filled with humility. And felt free to share it in real time, a rare moment of true authenticity.

> *emails* Posted: 24-Jun-2009 11:26:22 AM
> Stefan Words alone cannot convey my respect for what you have just done and for the intelligent insight you have gained from it. I am in awe. Lance Armstrong, when asked why he did it seven times, answered "to find out how deep - how good - I really am". In the Western Executive world that most of us inhabit, it is sadly true how little time we spend with ourselves - finding how good and how deep we really are. You just went to the wall to find out. Congratulations buddy. An amazing accomplishment. What a chapter for your story!!
> Doug Keeley

> Posted: 24-Jun-2009 10:09:13 AM
> Tremendous accomplishment Stefan! During a time when many of us are faced with extraordinary difficulties, you take on an additional monumental challenge! Your blogs clearly demonstrate the extensive personal insight you have received and will continue to receive as you reflect further. You probably do not realize the impact you have had on those of us that witnessed this adventure. If you see those around you improve themselves, know that you were a catalyst! I look forward to hearing more about your adventure story!
> Steve Phillips

PART 5
RECOVERING

CHAPTER 20

REENTRY

*Most people never run far enough
on their first wind to find out they've
got a second. Give your dreams all
you've got and you'll be amazed at
the energy that comes out of you*

—WILLIAM JAMES, PSYCHOLOGIST AND PHILOSOPHER

Reentry into my life was relatively easy, initially. I took the red-eye flight from Beijing, landed in Toronto at 6 a.m., and was at work by 8:30 a.m. I had a chance to recount and relive the story a few times. I was physically exhausted. It took a couple of weeks for my feet to heal and about a month for my body to want to do any type of exercise.

Not all of us had the same luck.

As Todd Handcock recalls: "While the pain of various blisters and muscle fatigue did make for some interesting physical challenges during the race, my biggest physical challenge came when I arrived back home in Hong Kong.

"With my right calf swollen to twice its normal size, I discovered that the swelling and pain were not muscular issues but rather a major infection that was threatening the leg's survival. I spent the next two weeks getting daily injections and consuming a cocktail of antibiotics to get the infection under control.

"So, with all of the drilling, threading, bleeding, infections, burning sun, hunger, lack of sleep, losing 18 pounds, and sheer exhaustion, was it worth it? Absolutely! It was a brilliant experience! Knowing now about the pain that had to be endured, would I have done it? No question. I would be at the starting line in a heartbeat."

Collateral Damage

It would be dishonest to say there was no collateral damage out of prepping and running the race. The chief damage was that I needed to get re-acquainted with my wife. It seems as though we had not been together. We had been living separate lives for far too long. I also needed to decide if my life had grown too full to have time for all my friends and acquaintances.

I quickly realized that I would have to recalibrate my level of patience for anything sounding like a complaint, especially from colleagues during the tough times we were still going through. The same applied to my children's whining. I also noticed I had become judgmental of people who were unwilling to pay the price to do or be at their best. I am working on practicing acceptance and being empathetic. We all have our own set of standards, goals, and expectations, and for the first time I understood that whatever others were up to was their own choice and in no way a reflection on me. Who was I to judge if they should always try to realize their potential and be at their best and continually strive toward it?

This may turn out to be the greatest lesson I will ever learn, especially as related to my wife and kids. Love the wife and kids you have, not the ones you want. I learned that I needed to relax and count my blessings instead of constantly pushing for more. The key is to follow the plan.

email Posted: 23-Jun-2009 01:59:47 PM
*Stefan, Thank you for sharing your journey and your 'learns'.
I doubt you ever will forget those life changing insights,*

but make sure to refer back to your logs on a regular basis as it can
be easy to slip back into your previous ways (especially the ones you've
recognized you'd prefer not to). Looking forward to hearing more
upon your return. Safe travels back.
Kenny Solway

I also found I struggled back in my old life because I no longer had a buffer. The end of Gobi was not just the end of a six-day race; it was the end of an intense six-month project in which I had shocked my body, faced the unknown head on, and experienced mental breakdowns and euphoria. Initially I experienced a kind of light case of post-partum blues. I experienced bouts of wonderment about how I had changed and others not.

Shortly after returning, I met with a couple of friends, Sean Shannon and Jim McKenzie, who had read my blogs and encouraged me to write a book. Others suggested I should present my experience live to inspire others to overcome their own adversity and find ways to thrive in a changing environment. I'm doing that now, and not only has it allowed me to anchor more deeply the experiences I learned in the Gobi, it also has inspired and touched others in a way I could not do in my day job as a CEO and executive recruiter. I have been humbled to see how my own experience has helped others along in their quest to overcome the hurdles they're facing. Slowly, I am stepping into a clearing, finding that powerful place where I could make more of a difference.

A Change of Persona

The most fascinating and unexpected development? I have somehow altered my public persona. Like most everyone else, I had allowed my work and societal roles to define me. After all, my work identity had been built across more than 20 years, during which I was essentially in the same role and company. But now, in the span of six months, my persona had shifted. People were relating to me no longer as just the headhunter, the go-to guy for career advice but also as the desert runner guy.

Having started my career in marketing at Procter & Gamble, and then in my next career being a person who advised people on managing their own personal brands, I was liberated and frightened by the velocity with which this "remake" happened to me. Now I can tell people with great certainty that their personal brand can be altered based on their present and future actions. They don't have to be a product of their past.

When I review why I signed up for Gobi, I see that all of my personal objectives were exceeded. In December 2008, I decided that 2009 would end something like this:

- *My first objective was to get fit. I wanted to finish 2009 the fittest I could be so I could have have greater stamina for dealing with business issues. Mission accomplished. I felt stronger than in 1984 when I went to the Olympic trials for windsurfing. I have more stamina and more projects on my plate than at any point before. I continue to work standing, and I still don't own a car.*

- *My second objective was to turn my relationship to work upside down, no longer allowing it to define who I am. Feeling high as a kite or upset based on business results and the economy is too hard a way to live. While 2009 turned out to be a terrible year, financially, I broke the pattern of the previous downturns and didn't let myself become emotionally defined by it. In fact, I think I became impervious to the emotional abyss I have been known to visit. I chose to no longer "be" my compensation, our revenue, or our profit. My commitment has not changed; the difference is that it stays at work when I leave for home. I can be more present to the rest of my life.*

- *My third objective was to create conversational capital to inspire myself, my colleagues, and the desperate people I interview every day. The Gobi project created laughter in the office and helped put things in perspective. I am now presenting my experience regularly as a speaker and it has opened up an opportunity to make a difference in other people's lives, which at times is more emotionally fulfilling than my day job. The project's visibility has also opened up business relationships that were not available to me before. Net result: In spite of a bad year financially I am filled with the feeling that 2009 was that watershed year that opened up other avenues for me, my firm, and family.*

- *My fourth objective was to reinvent the business to get some distance to drive innovation to a mature industry. Amazingly, during the course of 2009, I got involved in a project to unlock the acceleration of executives joining a new organization; this project may completely change my business. Our business is transactional, and this product could change how we get paid and therefore how our clients perceive us. Business rebounded in 2010; revenue went up 66 percent, and my own production was up 70 percent. I believe the Gobi was a critical component of my personal rebound.*

- *My fifth objective was to come out of an experience feeling invincible – having the sense that if I could do this, I could do anything. Tough to measure, but I would say the trappings related to "playing safe" have mostly disappeared; as a result of Gobi, I was poised to take on more risks and experience more from life, including failures. It is a cliché, but I've never felt more alive.*

- *My last objective was to do some good for the community. I decided to raise funds for NABS in order to help those in our industry who were in distress. I hoped to raise $25,000; I exceeded that target by 100 percent.*

Before boarding the flight back from Beijing, walking around in my airline slippers to let my feet heal, I had time to add the Gobi March to my list of Top 20 life events, knocking off the number 72, the best golf score I ever played with my partner David Smith back in the 90s (shallow I know, but golfers can relate). My thirst for other intense extraordinary experiences was palpable and inspired me to add many life projects to my bucket list, projects that would keep me living in full intensity. The list helped me. While I enjoy spontaneity, I prefer to see a future I can step toward. After all, I was 45, having lived half of my productive life. The future is not predictable, as I learned from my dad's sudden ill health and death.

All it took was an hour. I titled it my Gobi list (see appendix 4). I furiously wrote down all the places I wanted to see, the experiences I wanted to have, the things I wanted to learn, and the summits I wanted to reach and achieve. Then I attached a date to each: within a year, five years, and ten years. And I identified who I wanted to do each item with: my wife, family, mother, friends, business colleagues, or solo. As I boarded my flight, I started to think about my next project, now with a menu of more than a hundred dreams to choose from! I think the exercise helped my feet heal faster.

Twenty years from now, you will be more disappointed
by the things you didn't do than by the ones you did.

—MARK TWAIN

Since coming back, I've had fascinating conversations with people I know and with new ones I've met about the Gobi List, theirs and mine.

As expected, now that I had converted my dreams to a written list and then shared it with others, I found that many others shared some of the same dreams and aspirations. This, of course, generated connections and momentum toward bringing the projects to reality.

My list was the catalyst for conversations. And conversation, whether held with oneself or others, is where actions are birthed.

"Show it to me," said Heather MacLean and Kim Smithers, two Toronto women who have participated in eco-challenges before. I found out they, too, were interested in diving with whale sharks. One thing led to the next and Kim sent me a picture a month later of her with a monstrous whale in the background and the caption, "Done!" No doubt it wouldn't have happened without that conversation.

I always wanted to go extreme helicopter-skiing in Alaska. I came back and told my ski buddies, and they of course responded with, "We're in, just organize it!" Almost two years later, in April 2011, we did it. "The best ski day of my life" said Evan Siddall. Tackling incredibly steep terrain, it will be forever stamped in our memories.

I've been watching the Tour de France race for 20 years, shaking my head at the Alp and Pyrenees mountain stages that the riders conquer. I always wanted to ride up the famed mountain stages with my uncle Keith Carrier, who got into biking 30 years ago. Keith was my hero growing up; he built a great business, offered me a marketing job while I was in university, and routinely handed me a beating on the squash or badminton court or the golf links.

A few years back, Keith had heart problems that led him to a triple bypass and then an artificial heart valve. We thought climbing Alpe d'Huez would still be possible, but it turned out to be ill-advised for him. I happened to be in France in May 2011 and decided to be opportunistic and drove 600 kilometers for the thrill of trying it. The ascent alone was my most memorable hour and twenty minutes on a bike ever. I could feel my uncle with me on the way up, along with Lance Armstrong and other prominent cyclists as each of the 21 switchbacks is dedicated with a prominent sign to a former Huez stage winner.

Another item on my Gobi list was to be able to look back on my life and remember great memories of living abroad with my family. Having lived reasonably, I have always suppressed the idea. Too complicated, given our jobs, income, board roles, community commitments, and school for the kids. After discussing it, we threw caution to the wind and decided to incur all the financial and reputational risks and unforeseen issues that come with a transfer. We are moving to France as a family for a small part of 2012. The kids have started to research what they can do in Paris while my wife and I will be replenishing our souls while working there.

• • •

My friends Ernie and Louie decided there were more deserts to conquer and they convinced themselves, and later me, over an expensive Cabernet, that a group of three old guys could compete in the team competition in the Atacama Crossing, another RacingThePlanet race. So we registered as a team called Old Guys Rule for the March 2010 event.

Located in Chile, just south of Peru, the Atacama is the highest and driest desert on earth. In fact, not a single drop of rain has been recorded in known history in some parts where we ran. The Atacama delivered more than a few nosebleeds!

More than 160 competitors registered, including seven teams. The youngest runner was 18, and Laurence Brophy would provide all the inspiration we needed as the oldest runner at 78. We ran by ancient sacred Inca sites, close to where a 9,000-year-old mummy was excavated, and close to NASA's Mars rover test site. Not only was it be an amazing experience, I also got to knock off Buenos Aires and the Chilean wine region from my Gobi List of places to see.

In the Gobi, Kashi was being destroyed, and in Chile, one of the most devastating earthquakes in history hit the southern tip, bringing the country to a halt days before the race.

The best two teams were manned by current and former

British military officers. In multi-day events, anything can happen and our team ended up winning the race. Details to follow in a new book exploring how a team of middle-aged men found a way to overcome adversity and gel as a team.

At publishing time, I was leaving for Egypt with a group of eleven other including my mentor, Mehmet, to run the third of 4 Deserts/RacingThePlanet, called the Sahara Race. I will try to repeat a team win and provide on-the-ground support for eight rookies running their first desert and raise $100,000 for NABS along with them. This is a natural evolution of my journey, progressing from I (Gobi), to We (Atacama), to All (Sahara). I plan to hand over the baton and go for a rest after.

If you want to go quickly, go alone.
If you want to go far, go together.
—AFRICAN PROVERB

So what is your Gobi?

CHAPTER 21

TEN LESSONS
FROM THE DESERT

*R*unning is the greatest metaphor for life,
because you get out of it what you put into it.
–OPRAH WINFREY, TALK SHOW HOST

Never having spent as much time with myself as I did while
in the Gobi Desert, I had ample opportunity to reflect on
my experience. Following are my ten deepest Gobi Runner
lessons.

1. Gratitude Is the Key to Performance

As has often been said, where you are born has a lot to do
with your success. We are blessed to live in the free world.
I love traveling; in fact, I have a giant map at home with push-
pins marking the places I've been, making it obvious how
much of the world is still out there for me to see. Sometimes
it's when I leave Canada that I appreciate it the most. Seeing
the city of Kashi being destroyed against its inhabitants' will
was revolting. I'm more aware now of the incredible advantage I have by being Canadian. It is a story I need to share
more with my children, so they will be thankful for their
good fortune and live in a spirit of gratitude. It doesn't matter
where on the globe we are, when I and others from Canada
compete, the presence of our flag on our shirts guarantees

that we'll be greeted with open arms. I am now displaying my flag with more vigor inside my own country.

The human mind can scan either for what it likes or what it doesn't like. We all know that scanning for the positive in ourselves delivers a higher level of self-esteem and enables us to leverage our talents with confidence and face hurdles with more courage. Scanning for the positive in others creates appreciation and a deeper connection that yields trust. And trust magnetizes others to want to be around us and encourages them to be their best.

The breakthrough for me was learning, not only to face undesirable events, but to actually be grateful for them. This helped me vaporize the potential impact of almost all of the difficulties I faced. In fact, I started to welcome them and systematically turn them into learning opportunities. During the race, I cultivated a positive relationship with the wind, the heat, the rolling rocks, and the rivers; while these factors debilitated some, they became assets for me.

Being a neophyte runner, I had to endure serious setbacks, especially injuries. When I was told two months before the event that my shin splints and Achilles tendinitis would keep me from running the race, I had to embrace running in circles in the shallow end of a pool while floating to eliminate impact. I had ample opportunity to conclude the Gobi run wasn't meant to be; yet, despite vacillating at times, in time I chose to befriend the pool. Chris Davies chose to run in spite of losing his luggage. Kevin Lepsoe chose to carry on in spite of a banged-up leg. What they and I found was that willing yourself forward makes the journey that much more memorable. In fact, right now, fresh from a knee surgery, I am now heading to run in the Sahara. When asked if I'm going to be able to run, I'm answering: "Yes, I have been growing wings!"

Before leaving Canada for the race, I was blessed by how the race evolved from being a challenge to jumpstart me during a bad recession to being a means of giving to people in our industry who had fallen into hard times through raising support from hundreds of pledgers. At times of duress, these people's support carried me forward. The inbound emails in the cyber-tent often brought me – and others as they read the messages they were receiving – to tears.

I reframed my interpretation of the many hardships that we experienced during the race – including the rolling rocks and river crossings of day one, the heat of day two, and the wind of day four – converting them to an advantage. My mechanism for keeping my mind from straying to the negative was to laugh out loud. I was grateful for adversity and asked for more. Every time the elements turned nasty, I gained precious minutes, because I was running happy instead of sour.

On day one, I dug deep and relied on my inner strength to complete my first marathon in spite of adversities I wouldn't have faced running one in Boston or New York. I was internally focused, choosing to insulate myself from what went on with others. It was as if their struggles gave me wings. That day turned out to be a great athletic achievement for me, a top ten finish. Yet the other days were far more fulfilling because I learned to turn my focus outward. The tipping point was on day two when others helped me so generously after my pack broke. I began to clue into a feeling that I should do the same while competing, whether by sharing food, carrying someone's pack from the finish line to their tent, or just offering someone a massage. I waited for hours next to the finish line just to lend a hand for a few minutes by welcoming people home after their longer day.

Since coming back, I have been practicing random acts of generosity. True to the male paradigm, I find it difficult to be aware of my environment and be thoughtful toward others. I am naturally focused on my agenda and oblivious to pretty much everything else. I am a big gesture guy – I actually proposed to my wife while riding a white horse, yet I'm not so good with the small, daily stuff.

Making a spirit of gratitude my operating mantra put me at one with the desert. Operationalizing gratitude turned out to be the best policy during the race. For example, on day four, I thanked Kevin for passing me and showing me I was capable of trying to run him down. I didn't succeed in doing so, but losing to him in the context of an attitude of gratitude expanded my own success boundaries. My take-home learning was that this wasn't a defeat: it was a win.

Now I see that I must operationalize gratitude everywhere else: not only at work, but also at home, and in life in general. For example, my competitive spirit prompts me to see most things as binary in nature – as something I either win or lose. Winning produces a positive feeling, and losing too often does not. Get the promotion – I am happy. Win the project – happy. Lose the golf match – unhappy.

In business, I've been socialized to dislike the firms we compete against. Dislike? That's putting it mildly. I have related to the world too frequently in strict Darwinian terms, operating based on a fear of scarcity, a win/lose attitude, and the fervent belief that only the fittest deserve to survive. Now, however, instead of trampling on my competitors, I am learning that they are the ones who show us what we're made of, push us to innovate, force us to refine our business model, and invite us to work harder and smarter. Losing to them offers valuable lessons. If I had been without competitors in the desert, I would have walked! I have since paid more attention to my competitors in order to understand how and why they succeed. On most days in the desert, I expanded my ability to go faster, being pushed beyond my perceived capability. The current winding path the economy is taking out of recession is teaching me the same. In the desert, going fast required me to learn from a competitor or to collaborate with one, working for hours as a team to put distance on the field, pushing each other; this even extended to recovering together in camp.

I seem to recall that I was better at playing the corporate bongo drums to recognize people for doing good things or simply to encourage them along when life was less complex. I now see how it is even more important for me to do so when times are difficult.

The same goes for me at home, where I must cheer my daughters to their various finish lines, so they can face their obstacles productively, and repurpose the lessons they learn without too much scar tissue.

2. Good Things Happen When We Declare an Honorable and Lofty Goal

We all know that having a goal is a great start. But private goals are really just good intentions. I went public with the run and of course heard a few dissonant voices, but in general, the universe around me shifted to help me get there. At times, I wandered, and I needed others to hold me accountable. Just being asked how my training was doing helped me keep my focus. Going public, making the declaration of my intention via a website, not only drew me toward my goal, but also created public pressure on me to get it done.

When I look back, I can think of ten or so personal examples of creating a seemingly impossible goal and seeing it come to fruition a few years later, typically right on schedule. Don't get me wrong. I have fallen flat on my face, too, but I look at these as learning experiences.

Having a fundraising objective helped tether me to a higher purpose. Like running, most of life's activities can be solitary; running for others is not.

3. One Step at a Time Is What It Takes to Get There

I had asked my mentor Donna how she managed to run the Gobi given she also was not a runner at the time. Her simple answer: "I did it one step at a time." She advised me never to think about the magnitude of it all. When running in the desert was just too much, I thought about making it to the next 10-kilometer checkpoint. Or continuing for the next ten minutes. Or the next flag. Or, when there was nothing left, just one more step.

When friends questioned my sanity about running six marathons in five days, I responded that it was just one race. Mehmet had advised that I could shift my perception of the long day by thinking of it not as an enormous 85-kilometer double marathon but as the last major run of five days. "By then you are closer to the finish line than the start line," he said. "It is just one day, Stéfan." It worked. Whatever bite size you can chew is the right increment to think about. I ran more than 1,500 kilometers while training. I would have been overwhelmed by the challenge had I thought or known that it would take that much running to prepare.

When he helps athletes recover from their injuries, my chiropractor, Dr. Kazemi, always breaks the rehabilitation down into the smallest possible steps; this helps the athletes see short-term progress as opposed to the macro view of injury and setback.

The same applies to building a career, a team, and a company. I needed to establish a solid foundation with a vision, mission, and values, and then layer on the strategies and tactics later. Raising children is the same; you do it one conversation at a time.

The economy is still challenging, but I will get through it by focusing on the elements I can control. I tend to want to rush things through. At times it works, but more often than not, luck, or a good economy, or the right circumstances have more to do with it than the plan.

4. The Winning Team Is Often Not the Fastest Group of Individuals

The team competition offered the possibility that less gifted runners could in fact win the battle if they behaved as a unit, an inspired philosophy we leveraged later while running the Atacama crossing as a team.

In the Gobi, Team Cohesion was aptly named. It was composed of Giles Timms and Gareth Hicks, both of them British military officers, and Sophie Collett, a physiotherapist. These three had an established leadership system, solid conflict-resolution protocols, and a high level of trust. Some of the other teams had faster runners but failed to stick together. They were exhibit A of the difference between a team and a group of individuals. Almost all of the teams in the Gobi imploded; they were unable to reconcile their differences, handle their setbacks, and alter their expectations of each other. A team faster than Cohesion met that fate on the first day.

As Giles puts it, "We discussed in detail the use of iPods and post-stage administration with recovery and re-hydration, all the while agreeing to constantly move at the fastest speed that the slowest member could manage. That in itself required a lot of discipline. Personally speaking, as a 2:48 marathoner, I was regularly chomping at the bit and somewhat wistful that I couldn't be competing for a top ten slot. But I quickly and easily put that from my mind, knowing that the selfish/vainglorious motivation would not feel so satisfactory when I had to look myself in the shaving mirror. I asked Sophie to join Gareth and me, and we undertook the race as a team ... There was no question of ever splitting it down. Tactically, it was all about damage-limitation."

Giles says that he had trashed his feet in 2008 during the Marathon des Sables, and in Gobi was determined that no one on the team would meet that same fate.

"The 'more haste, less speed' adage was running through

our brains throughout. It was simply maintenance of a strong pace from the outset of each day until anyone began to slow, and then simply cajoling them and pulling them up to as fast a pace as possible."

For her part, Sophie says she was constantly aware that she was "running with two gifted runners, both of whom had been much faster in a previous race. It's a daunting prospect knowing that you are the weakest link in a team with two other guys. It also presents a change in the way you race. A successful team, I feel, is one that really works together and supports each other. Running within 20 meters of two other people at all times and therefore spending all day every day running those kind of distances in such tough environments is a real test of strength and character in a very different way to doing it individually."

She says that while they were by no means the fastest team on paper, "our ability to relate and listen to each other and work together helped us make up this disadvantage and overall be the strongest team. It was hard, though. There are times when you just want your own space or one of you is tired and wants to slow down and the others feel strong and want to push on, and it does make it tough to keep that team cohesion. Competing as a team really is a great challenge and all of us felt very proud in our achievement of completing it so successfully together. We went out with the mindset that we wanted to enjoy the race and our time together. We had no expectations of winning; we just wanted to do well for ourselves as a team. We made sure we were focused on encouragement, and shared our food/drinks, and added levity and fun chats for a moral boost."

5. Comfort Is Not the Same as Happiness

My mentor, Mehmet, who won one of these races, says, "Think of when you were happiest. Were any of you eating potato chips sitting on a couch? Of course not. So get moving."

I saw desert children happily play soccer with a stitched leather ball filled with straw. Mine can get cranky when the Wii or DS isn't working properly. I get upset when the remote needs batteries! It's time for me to live as if less is in fact more. Endurance events like the Gobi March are growing; they're part of a reaction to the comfort culture we have created for ourselves. After a while, another plasma TV just isn't going to do it for you. A challenge is far more nourishing.

Wanting or needing more is what our Western culture is all about. One of the racers, Kevin Lepsoe, knows this well.

"In Hong Kong, there's always someone who has more. I've learned to be thankful for what I have. I think everyone who can afford to pay for this race (and the equipment) has plenty to be thankful for. A race like this helps you recognize what's important and what you can do without. What you really need is health, family, friends, and time to spend with them. I've 'prescribed' this race to many people that I know are looking for a bit of direction – coincidentally many guys/ girls in their 30s who've 'succeeded' in a professional context but forgotten the existence of a world outside."

Most individuals in the Gobi were going through some sort of event in their lives that put them there. It was clear that the discomfort we experienced became a symbol of some sort of awakening.

For me, comfort is the buffer zone between fear of failure and fear of success. I always knew I was afraid of failure. I hate failing and I work hard at not failing. It is what has given me most of what I have. But during the race I was confronted with the possibility of actually winning. Strangely, in a sense struggling is my comfort zone. I know that I almost always find a way to kick into another gear and find a way out. In the desert I saw more clearly than ever that when I do well, I am uncomfortable and am almost apologetic about it. A misplaced sense of humility robs me of my own power.

It has been fascinating for me to become aware of

what stopped me. For five days "I danced like nobody was watching" and then I stopped. It is a subject I am exploring right now, hoping to feel worthy of winning – of removing this self-imposed ceiling altogether, or at least raising it higher.

6. Being Vulnerable Enables Growth

As a business leader, you are taught to project that you're in control, that you have the answers. The adverse conditions of the desert removed the protective shell that I had learned to carry. I became more vulnerable and my authenticity was there for all to witness.

I rarely choose to go to that authentic place because I perceive that too much is at risk. Yet in connecting with people who enjoyed the authenticity of my blog or my presentations on the Gobi, I have grown as a person, learning to acknowledge that I didn't have all the answers. I want to become that kind of leader.

Vulnerability also invited more active learning into my life; some people, for the first time, have stepped forward to let me have it.

7. Playing Safe Leaves Us Feeling Comfortable and at Times Empty

I changed my strategy on the long day and forgot what got me there. I would have had the satisfaction of winning the race among Canadians and my age group if I had decided to run my race as opposed to hanging with my key direct competitors. True, I might have gotten injured, but I spent too much time looking around, looking behind in the first half of it, running and marking others. I ambushed myself. While I did win overall, I didn't win the long day itself among Canadians – which I could have, for no other reason than to do it.

A good lesson for me in life or work is to never take my foot off the gas pedal, especially when I'm doing well.

I disrespected the last 10 kilometers and fumbled. The current economic slowdown will help solidify this lesson.

8. A Difficult Journey Grows Our Adversity Quotient

I grew up an only child – I didn't have to fight for my share of spaghetti! Along the way I became competitive and driven. Or was it that I felt I was entitled? A previous divorce, losing my father, and other personal experiences around challenges helped me to build my resilience. As CEO of a service company with a commoditized product, I learned to be even more durable. But have I really faced true adversity? There is no doubt I am hardier today than I was before running in the desert. Knowing that I paid the price of training, showed up, finished, and competed hard when I had hundreds of reasons to quit – these are life skills I can now summon to my side in other situations.

Self-doubt is forever present when you take on a project like this. Just as the recession was threatening our business, the desert told me it would hurt me – it was just a matter of when and how badly. You're not quite sure what the price will be, but you know it's coming, probably just around the next sand dune.

Completing what you thought was impossible is a glorious moment of freedom and personal renewal. If I, a non-runner, could do this, I can know that I can do anything I set my mind to. Every Gobi participant shared in that experience and personal breakthrough; it was no doubt the toughest challenge they had ever undertaken, and at the same time, most completed it.

Todd Handcock says it best.

"Quitting was just not something that went through my mind. Not when I was drilling my toenails to relieve the pain from the blisters beneath them. Not when at kilometer 15 of the long day I found raw back bacon blisters across the back of both heels. Not when crossing 30 kilometers of nothing to step on but baseball-sized rocks. And not while clambering through the oven of a 45-degree-Celsius canyon. The thought of quitting just never came into play."

Sometimes, adversity manifests itself in the smallest of details. I suffer from the grave illness of perfectionism. I was confronted with my inner voice, which, as it turns out, likes to criticize more than support me. I might say the right thing in public – "you can do this" – while inside saying exactly the opposite. I have made headway in becoming a better friend to myself. I have expanded my ability to handle the criticisms and judgments I direct at myself, others, and my circumstances, and detach myself a bit and use them as learning opportunities. Now, when the inner critic (let's call him Eddy) flares, I thank him (yes, he is male) for sharing so generously. Eddy shuts down quickly when no one indulges him in his wise comments.

After running 70 kilometers for nine and a half hours, I somehow ran the fastest 15 kilometers of my life. I now know as a fact that I have a tougher mind and a stronger heart than I realized. I was blind to what I could ask my body and mind to do. Since then, when I train, work, or play with the kids and I feel like I've had enough, I definitely know I'm kidding myself. They are just feelings, which I can easily choose to disregard.

9. The Journey's Means Justify the End

I have always lived by the-end-justifies-the means maxim. Starting anything gets me excited. Then at times I go for a long half-measure doze. Then I see a finish line and I like to complete and sprint to it. Suffering from this affliction means I'm not at my best during the journey and that an unhealthy, disproportionate amount hinges on winning or losing.

It's much better to be happy on the journey; the end lasts but a day, or a few seconds. I've known this intellectually but could never put myself fully in the present so it would occur that way in my mind. Now, when I wake up, my first thought (after stretching in bed) is that I'm lucky. I'm alive!

I found a way to change hardened habits during my training. Being creative brought freedom. Creativity allowed me to be "in the moment" as opposed to sleepwalking through the training, which I equated to life's long dry spells. At work now, I make a point to review some of my more traditional habits, even the winning ones, and turn them on their heads just to keep things interesting. This is important for me. Unlike most professionals who have the opportunity for renewal through a promotion or a career change, I have been in the same job for a long time. For example, I am dedicating time to enjoying the process of preparing and pitching for new business as opposed to making it all about winning.

10. We Choose Our Feelings

There is what happens, and what we decide it means. We have control over the latter. Some people can get there quickly, others need time for processing. I have made one too many decisions based on how I felt, responding too quickly to what life handed me. Some of these choices have altered my life's outcomes.

Ernie would likely concur. He was injured partly through not reinterpreting quickly enough his upset about our misaligned expectations. Six months of work, pulverized. Thankfully, I witnessed it and it caused me to welcome the wind, the heat, the rivers, the rocks, the mountains, and choose to laugh my way through them. It was the right choice for me at that moment. I did struggle to adapt to some of the more personal hurdles, such as my backpack breaking down, and getting lost. Every time I failed to adapt, I lost my focus, fell, or made mistakes. But I learned to snap out of feeling victimized.

More important, in Ernie's case, was the decision he made upon returning from the Gobi, which was to head to the Atacama. His springing forward was contagious; he was more prepared than we were and led our team from the front to first place under extreme conditions.

His handling of the Gobi helped me explore areas in my life where I am a victim. Those areas and that mentality no longer seep into the office and my home.

The study of the brain is now so advanced, there are numerous tools available to rewire it for success, happiness, and abundance.

APPENDICES

MENTORING AND VISUALIZATION

Two effective approaches I honed as a teenager were to accelerate my own development through mentoring and visualizing the finish line.

Mentoring was likely out of necessity; I neither had an older sibling nor parents who were into sports as I was. Also, I skipped grade 6 in school and found myself from age 11 and on with kids a year older. I didn't fit in and struggled to keep up athletically, in addition to other typical adjustment issues. While my parents were incredibly encouraging, I had the experience of being on my own.

Never blessed with great balance as a tall kid, visualization just came from trying to mentally rehearse making ski or skateboard moves to try to keep up with my more mature friends. Deconstructing the physics helped me to understand how to position my body at the right time.

In the early 80s, windsurfing was in its heyday and I got into it. I was looking for a positive outlet to pour my energy into as I had just been evicted from my golf club permanently for having had one too many temper tantrums. I wanted to get competent fast and I felt the best way to get there was to search for the best windsurfers I could find and learn from them. My parents hoped the breeze would have a cooling effect on my temperament. I was 18.

I wasn't really interested in reinventing the wheel – my attitude is, if it can be done well, learn it from someone who has reached mastery. Once competent, I could add in my own style and tweak it to what worked for me. I craved burning through the learning milestones by following better sailors.

Over time and unbeknownst to Eric Graveline, then Canada's very young national champion, I sort of "recruited" him as my mentor. It made for an unusual relationship; I was 18 and he was 14! I asked him a hundred questions about the sport and modeled my approach around his. I took notes and read them at night. I even considered becoming vegan as he suggested my erratic, tantrum moods on the water might be affected by the excessive amounts of red meat I ate. Over time we became friends. On numerous occasions, I got a chance to train with him, which was a privilege; Eric was training to secure Canada's first and only berth as our Olympian at the 1984 Los Angeles Games where windsurfing would be a demonstration sport. In late March he would be on the frigid waters of Lake St. Louis in Montreal every day, sleet, hail, snow, or shine, to prepare for the Olympic trials to be held in May. So I joined in.

He would do hundreds of tacks and jibes to perfect the maneuvers that can cost you one to two seconds each, even though in a race you may only do fifty tacks and probably under ten jibes. He was completely rehearsed; whatever would happen in a race, he had repeated the movement thousands of times and could react swiftly. I did what he did, just not as well. This included reading the same books on strategies and tactics and dropping the red meat, too. While my friends may have visualized scoring the winning goal and winning the Stanley Cup, or holing a 6-foot putt for a win at Augusta, I wanted to be at one with water, wind, and a sailboard, and cross the finish line first.

We both went to the Olympic trials, and of course my young mentor won and got to represent Canada in LA at age 16. He had visualized winning and being at the Olympics. The by-product of training with him was extraordinary for me; in my third year windsurfing, I accomplished what would probably have taken twice as long: I won the Quebec Championships, placed second at the Nationals, and 20th at the World Championships in my weight class. I had picked the right mentor and visualized the race from start to finish.

The world works in mysterious ways Eric paid me forward with his mentoring, and I was able to repay him by gifting him all of my course notes and essays when he chose to do a B. Comm. at McGill University, the same program I had taken.

All athletes discuss the power of visualization. Michael Jordan has said he did more free throws than anyone else. In his mind, that is! When you've done it in your mind, it comes to you a lot easier in real life. Like others who have that belief, I have greatly benefited from visualizing the future I want before it occurs. There are even studies that demonstrate that your body twitches the same way during mental rehearsal as it would during an actual event.

Planning a career is no different. The main reason I chose to work at Mandrake was the learning opportunity that the Chair, Harold Perry, offered me. I camped in his office for two weeks when I joined to witness how he expertly handled a myriad of issues. At the end of two weeks, I knew more about the recruiting business than most people do after three years. And planning a race in the desert is the same.

Before undertaking the training, I wrote a descriptive account of what the race would feel like, look like, and end like. I would seek mentors to learn the essentials of training and seek their help to fill in the blanks on the "look part" of the terrain, life in camp, as well as about the pain I would experience. Once injured, I even mentally learned to run by rehearsing the video footage in my mind, either through meditation or training in slow motion in the pool, as I was unable to actually run.

The approach I used for this is the one we use at NEXCareer, our career transition service. In an exercise, with a client, we transport ourselves to their career finish line. We use words like: "Assume it is 2020 and you are looking back at your amazing career, toasting yourself on a great success." We work with clients to have them pick a specific location that would bring them joy as they look back (mine would be the back bowls of Whistler), and then ask them to visualize the company where they worked and the title they held at the end of their great career. And then we reverse engineer the full travelogue of their career. The net result helps them leap toward their future as opposed to continuing on the path they were on.

In my case, I locked in on a vision of completing the 85-km-long fifth day of the race and looking back with pride at having given it my best, celebrating having pushed myself to a level beyond anything I had previously imagined. Basically the exercise was to see the whole project, from end to beginning, at a granular level only your creative side can create. It would raise my ability to overcome challenges and conquer projects I once would have thought impossible.

I never chose a specific finish number, I just wanted to finish, exhausted but proud, knowing I would have had a personal breakthrough and in some way changed the course of my life for the better. In fact, it might put into perspective my work problems brought on by the economy, making them laughing matters rather than issues that would own me.

Somehow, in my life, with almost everything I have experienced, acquired, accomplished, and failed at, I saw it before it happened. Yes, I can visualize failing as well as I can succeeding, as my golf partners can attest. In fact, I delight them by asking them how far the hazards are as opposed to focusing on hitting the ball straight.

Unbeknownst to me, the picture I painted in my mind would completely come true during the race, a self-fulfilling prophecy, until the self-doubt that seeped in on the rest day when 99 percent of the hard work was done.

RUNNING GEAR

Gear selection is very complex because you carry everything on your back. It is a puzzle in which every ounce of food is optimized to deliver the greatest caloric boost. You must test each item, see its impact, and assess its taste. The majority of the food is dehydrated, to be mixed with water. I started another whiteboard in my war room at home. The pre-requisite was to show the medical crew that you carried 2,000 calories of food per day. The weight is up to you. The only testing actually taking place is to demonstrate that you actually are carrying your own food and that it is at least the required minimum. The world of clever cheats never sleeps.

As runners around the world have started to take desert ultra marathons seriously, and have derived sponsorship benefits from placing well at these events, a trend has developed where a "friend" who acts as a mule, without podium aspirations, carries your food to lighten your load. Now, the top three runners and teams in categories are subject to a spot check when they cross the finish line.

In research, I learned that most people, especially newbies, over-packed food; so I chose to under-pack, keeping the food to a bare minimum. Because I eat more than most people, I actually planned to run out of food early and scavenge as others learned their mistake. As it turned out, my friend Louie became my favorite mule – he had over-packed beautiful sausages. But it did make him the most popular runner. This is what the food looked like:

Breakfast Food	Running Food	Dinner Food
2 Lasagnas 470g	To be equally split for each of the 4 legs of a day (2x for long day)	Katmandu Beef 660g
Spaghetti 400g	Sport Beans 100cal x 4bags/day	Satay Beef 1120
Chicken Teriyaki 560g	Jerky Stick 1/day	Granola 720g
Eggs 440g	Nuun Electrolites 4/day	Teriyaki Beef 600g
Chili 580g	Shot Bloks 2/day	Pasta 840g
Burrito 500g	Salted Almonds 4 bags/day	Muesli 760g
	Power Gel half a pack/day	
	Post race: Cytomax Recovery drink 2 bags	
Total 3420g	**Total 5288g**	**Total 4760g**
	Total 12,000 cals	

Picking the gear is equally challenging; every mandatory piece of equipment is to be evaluated for greatest performance with the least weight. They included:

Mandatory	Optional
Hat or Cap, Sunglasses, Jacket, Shorts, Fleece hat, Gloves, Shirts, Shoes, Sunscreen, Blister kit, Meds, Alcohol gel, Backpack, Sleeping bag, Head lamp and back up, Compass, Safety pins, Nationality patches, Whistle, Survival blanket, Knife, Red flashing light, Electrolytes, Food	**Which I took:** Slippers, Gaiters, Lip Sunscreen, Tin cup, Eating utensils, water bottles, Sleeping pad, Headgear, Socks, Zip lock bags, Wet wipes, Toothbrush/paste, Wristwatch, iPod, Solar panel, Camera, Ripped pages of magazines **Which I didn't:** Insect repellent, Tissues, GPS

Needless to say, while it would seem simple to choose what to bring, a lot of thought and consideration went into every piece, resulting in countless shopping visits to the Salomon corporate store, Mountain Equipment Coop, the Running Room, and Running Free.

TRAINING DETAILS

This is the six-month program I used, increasing distance about 10 percent per week from a 15-mile start, and increasing a weighted backpack up to 30 pounds.

To lighten up on this calendar, use kilometers instead. On the long days and high-mileage weeks, I broke the day into two runs to ease through it.

Week	Run Target	Walk Target	TTL Target	Target Weight
	Miles	Miles	Miles	Pounds
1	15	15	30	0
2	20	15	35	0
3	22	15	37	5
4	25	15	40	8
5	28	15	43	8
6	31	15	46	10
7	34	15	49	10
8	38	15	53	15
9	42	15	57	15
10	46	15	61	15
11	51	15	66	20
12	56	15	71	20
13	56	15	71	20
14	61	15	76	25
15	61	15	76	25
16	66	15	81	25
17	56	15	71	30
18	66	15	81	30
19	71	15	86	30
20	75	15	90	30
21	85	15	100	30
22	55	15	70	25
23	35	15	50	20
24	15	15	30	15
25	0	15	15	0
Race			**150**	**25**

APPENDIX 4

GOBI LIST CHART   What's your Gobi List?

THINGS TO				BY			WITH WHOM			
See	Experience	Accomplish	Learn	2012	2015	2020	Solo	Spouse	Family	Friends

CPSIA information can be obtained at www.ICGtesting.com
Printed in the USA
LVOW12s0059130515

438209LV00032B/1512/P